Once again Peg Bracken, whose warm art and cool comments make her text as delicious as her recipes, has taken the plight of the cooking-haters to heart and rescued them with a dozen delightful —and useful—chapters. There's an introduction, as an hors d'oeuvre, and an Index to the Appendix, as a souvenir menu.

Among the tidbits she serves forth are:

Alone, Cooking If (Eating with Your Shoes Off)

Anticlimax, The Daily 30 Entrees for the Simple-
minded & the Pure in Heart)

Dinner, Couldn't We Take Them Out to? (But
Sometimes You Can't)

Knowledgeable People, Stealing from (I Seen Her
When She Done It but I Never Left On)

Picnic, Going on a (What Ever Happened to Potato
Salad?)

Specialty, the Regional or Foreign (I Guess You
Always Lose a Little in the Translation)

And that, literally, is only the half of it.

Peg Bracken's

Appendix

to The

I Hate to Cook Book

with over 140 recipes and
323 afterthoughts

Drawings by
Hilary Knight

A FAWCETT CREST BOOK

Fawcett Publications, Inc., Greenwich, Conn.
Member of American Book Publishers Council, Inc.

THIS BOOK CONTAINS THE COMPLETE TEXT OF THE ORIGINAL HARDCOVER EDITION.

A Fawcett Crest Book reprinted by arrangement with Harcourt, Brace & World, Inc.

Copyright © 1966 by Peg Bracken.
All rights reserved, including the right to reproduce this book or portions thereof.

Library of Congress Catalog Card Number: 60-101919

PRINTING HISTORY
Harcourt, Brace & World edition published October 19, 1966
First printing, July 1966
Second printing, September 1966
Selection of the Better Homes and Gardens Family Book Service, November 1966

First Fawcett Crest Printing, October 1967

Published by Fawcett World Library
67 West 44th Street, New York, N. Y. 10036
Printed in the United States of America

Dedicated, with love,
to my daughter
JOHANNA

ACKNOWLEDGMENTS

My special thanks to Mary McClintock Bosch, a strong shoulder and a good cook; to Mary Margaret Short; to Parker Edwards.

My gratitude, as well, to Frances and Edward Page, for the peace of mind they gave me as well as the Wolfe Eggs; and to Hattie and Jack Pepper, for their interest and their ingredients.

Contents, Table of

Apologia,
More or Less of an

Early one spring morning a year ago, I was awakened by a strong urge to write a second Cook Book—an urge as astonishing as it was disconcerting. I had long ago said my last word on the subject, or so I felt. Too, I was well into the writing of another book, purposefully as far away from kitchens as you can go.

It is true that I've frequently been asked when I would write the *I Still Hate to Cook Book*. But my sincere reply was usually, Never. Or—for variation, perhaps—when the cows come home. On skate boards. The fact that I still hate to cook was or should have been, I thought, self-evident. You don't recover from hating to cook, any more than you get over having big feet.

Why, then, this compulsion? I had to muddle it over in my mind.

One primary reason, I presently suspected, was the people who have cooked and eaten gallantly of the recipes in the first book[1] and who have written to me or talked to me about it. More, they have mentioned ideas they think should have appeared in it, as well as some areas I hadn't touched upon: cooking for one's self, cooking and dieting, and several others. Most of them seemed to me eminently sensible, for

---

[1] *The I Hate to Cook Book,* Harcourt, Brace & World, Inc., 1960. Fawcett Crest paperback edition, 1966.

we who hate to cook usually see eye to eye, and even aye to aye.

Another reason is that in the past few years I have unintentionally made some culinary discoveries, mainly involving prepared foods and easier ways to do things, which supersede things in the first book.

I am well aware that to skilled and ardent cooks my innocent pride in these findings will resemble that of the little man who showed up at the Patent Office last year with his new invention, designed for talking across distances, which he had named "the telephone."

But honesty must out. If these things come as news to even a few, I will consider my efforts well spent.

Then there was another factor. I've noticed that some misconceptions are being disseminated by new or newish cookbooks.

To take only one, consider those odd little books that keep pairing Cooking with Sex. For instance, how to cook him a Sunday morning breakfast that will make him propose. Then they go into such things as broiled curried orange slices.

Now we who hate to cook wouldn't dream of cooking Sunday morning breakfast for a man until he *has* proposed. Preferably in writing. Even then, it will be good old-fashioned bacon and eggs.

Indeed, this whole tie-up of food and sex has been overdone. They don't have all that much to do with each other. Through the years, we who hate to cook find that there's usually a nice man around somewhere whether we are in one of our noncooking periods or in one of our totally noncooking periods.

(Though it's possible that cooking and sex have something to do with each other in rather an inverse way. I know a man who blissfully insists that his wife make her own kind of blackberry jam every summer, the kind, he says, that you pour on the toast. You see?)

But mainly what was bothering me, I do believe, was the 20-20 hindsight with which I have long been blessed. A number of things never got into *The I Hate to Cook Book* because—like the clams in a recent clam chowder—I forgot to put them in. I think these things have been kicking ever since at the floor of my subconscious and making me uncomfortable.

So this is truly an Appendix, and, in my case, it had to come out. It contains few cross references, however, or—at least—they're as good-natured as possible in view of the material at hand.

Now, perhaps, I shall be at peace. May you be at peace, too.

—PEG BRACKEN

CHAPTER 1

Alone, Cooking if

EATING WITH YOUR SHOES OFF

". . . In the middle of the woods
Lived the Yonghy-Bonghy-Bo. . . ."
—EDWARD LEAR

It is a barefooted fact that cooking and eating alone can be remarkably relaxing. There is no one to comment on the fact that it's meatloaf again and no dessert, or to interrupt with larger issues when you want to talk about smaller ones, and vice versa.

Not that it is completely clear sailing, even so. One of the reefs that can hang you up, when you hate to cook, is that some of the best things are big.

For instance, an important thing to know about cooking for yourself is how to cook a Prime Rib for one person.

When you know how to do this, you can have a couple of slabs of lovely juicy rosy-rare roast beef* whenever you like, without wallowing in leftover meat, or paying too much for one slice of it in a restaurant.

We'll come to that in a minute, after we look at the problem itself—the problem of cooking to stay alive when there's no one there to see, and you can accordingly get by with anything.

The problem hasn't really been solved by several recent books on the subject, which tell you how to make Pickled-Beet-and-Macaroni Salad for One, or Ox Tongue with Raisin Sauce for One, and that sort of thing.

These books don't get to the heart of it. Their authors, who obviously like to cook, have no idea what people who don't are willing to put up with, in exchange for the sheer joy of not cooking.

While there are recipes in this chapter, they are recipes of a different kind. The truth is, anyone who has trouble getting the lead out of her lingerie to cook for other people will find it all but impossible to do so for herself. The minimal cooking done in these situations is truly breath-taking.

I know an elderly lady whose breakfast is whole-wheat toast, bacon, and coffee; whose lunch is a vitamin pill with a Metrecal chaser; and whose dinner is an Old-Fashioned and something frozen, whatever she bumps into first in her fair-sized frozen-food compartment. She's the healthiest elderly lady you ever saw, too, as I happen to know, because she is my mother.

What she relies on to make those frozen dishes extra-palatable is a remote-control box for her television set, to cut off the commercials. (She finds it impossible to eat with all those people whining about their underarm odor and their dandruff.)

I also know a man who lives alone—hates to cook—and never tires of frozen spinach soufflé, which is fortunate, because that's all he ever has for dinner at home besides a pan-broiled chop or a steak. Sometimes he pours canned cheese sauce on the soufflé. Not always.

And I know a girl who leans heavily on eggs. Hard-boiled. Soft-boiled. Scrambled. Or, in rare moments of culinary enterprise, in a Spanish omelet. She simmers, in butter, some

---

* Or unlovely gray-brown dried-up roast beef if you prefer yours overdone.

onion, green pepper, and chopped fresh tomato (I believe that's where the Spanish comes in). Then she pours it over the omelet.

I asked her if she didn't get tired of eggs, and she cackled that she did, but they were still better than cooking.

—But enough of case histories, and back to the Prime Rib.

BACHELOR'S BEEF
or, How to Cook a Prime Rib for One

Ask the butcher for 1 rib of a standing rib roast. This will weigh around two and a half pounds.

It's important that you freeze it, because it must be roasted frozen. So wrap it in freezer foil and do so. (You should have thought of this yesterday.)

Next day or next month, an hour and a half before you want to eat, take it out, unwrap it, and rub it all over with garlic, if you like garlic, and then with a tablespoon of salad oil or olive oil.

Stand it on its side in a baking pan, propped against two scrubbed or peeled baking potatoes.

Roast it at 400° for one hour and twenty-five minutes if you like it rare; ten minutes more if you like it fairly well done. Let it stand five minutes before you slice it.

I did this one night when I had a guest. There was enough left over for good cold beef the next night and several sandwiches thereafter, which I consider a good bargain.

Other than the Prime Rib, meat is easy for the person who cooks and eats alone. The broiled or pan-broiled steak (from T-bone to Minute), the chop, the ham slice, the sausage, and the hamburger take care of most situations when you're meat-minded.

Still, hamburger can pose a problem, as illustrated by the case of a friend of mine. Several months ago she bought and froze two pounds of ground chuck, thinking some day she'd make a meat loaf. But she could never remember to thaw it in time, and so she always had something else. At last reports, the frozen chuck was still there, and when she moves, the next renter will probably take it over with the apartment. (And he'd better read the information on page 53.)

A good thing to do before you freeze ground meat is to flatten it between pieces of waxed paper. Flatten it into a big ¾-inch-thick sheet of meat, or into individual patties. Either way, it thaws much faster, and you can then reshape it as you like.

Three ways with hamburger

Certainly there are hundreds of hamburger variations, but the Plain or Classic is still best for day-in day-out wear. A good easy system is this:

Mix ground round lightly with
a pinch of minced onion flakes
a dash of Ac'cent (MSG)
1 teaspoon beef bouillon, powdered, or a crumbled cube.

If you want to be positive your hamburger will be moist, add a teaspoon of water. Logically enough, this will see to it. But I don't know why it shouldn't be moist anyway if the meat is all right and you don't overcook it.

Shape this into a rather thick cake—1½ inches—and put it in a very hot iron skillet in which you've sprinkled some salt. No fat. Pan broil it at high heat, about five minutes per side, depending on how pink you like it in the middle.

The second way is to chop plenty of carrots, celery, and onion into the ground meat before you shape it into a patty. This is minor health insurance for people who resist vegetables. Then cook it the same way.

The third way is

POOR LONELY MAN'S POIVRADE

(Which you will like if you like pepper, and pepper steak, but won't if you don't. Pepper steak or *Steak au Poivre* is a yes-and-no proposition.)

Crush a tablespoonful of whole peppercorns with a blender or potato masher or wooden-spoon handle or pestle, whatever you have. Then roll the ground-meat patty in it so it's thoroughly coated, and pan broil it in butter. When it is done, salt the patty, put a little more butter in the pan and a tablespoon of dry vermouth (or other dry white wine), mix it around, pour it over the patty, and eat it.

Before we get any farther into the pantry, let's list here some equipment you will probably enjoy having:

A rack or stand for books and newspapers—the sort that holds them open—in case you decide to dispense with the television set altogether and read, which you may do with never a by-your-leave. Indeed, one of the blessings of solitary dining is its engaging informality. I often think of my grandmother, one of whose pleasures it was, when alone, to take out her teeth and eat ice cream.

A good frozen-food knife with a strong serrated edge.

A grade-A can opener. Electric ones are fine if you can stand the noise.

A good supply of varied bottled cocktails or apéritifs, if you like one before dinner. A Sidecar or a Daiquiri can be a pleasant change from plain spirits.

Vitamin pills. It's best to have your doctor's word here. Otherwise you'll probably waste money on vitamins you don't need. Vitamins seem to come in and go out like the tides, and it's hard to remember which ones are passé and which are currently hot.

Now for some other mainstays besides meat.

As indicated earlier, the reluctant solo cook is rather a creature of habit, who tends to major in one—and only one—of several eating patterns.

1. The English Muffin with Something on It
2. The Egg with Something under It
3. The Milk Shake with Something in It
4. The Soup with Something beside It
5. The Baked Potato with Something over It

That is, when the chips are down and the freezer contains mainly what you don't feel like thawing or eating, it will be one of these you revert to. So let us take a brief look at each one.

1. The English Muffin

For English Muffin you may read Toast or Hamburger Bun or French Roll, though I prefer good English muffins, which are generally available and freeze well.

In fact, you can read Open-Faced Sandwich here and be perfectly correct. If you prefer a sandwich closed-faced, you can put the other muffin half or bread slice on top. But there's no reason to unless you're going to put it in your pocket and take it somewhere, for it's only starchier and not so attractive.

The first step with your English muffin is the same: slice it with a sharp knife. Don't tear it with a fork, as purists would have you do, because you're going to toast it in the toaster.

Just one fork-torn English muffin can make an unbelievable pile of crumbs.

When it's toasted, butter it, and (2) place something on it, whatever you can find that seems likely. Then (3) top it with something else, and (4) slide it under the broiler for a moment. Step 4 is often unnecessary, and is mainly employed to give the illusion of something hot. The combinations in the following list in which broiling really improves things are marked with a B.

Arrangements are endless, of course, and some are better than others. It depends on what is in one's rather erratically stocked pantry.

TOP:	shrimps	any smoked fish
MIDDLE:	hard-boiled egg in mayonnaise	cream cheese or sour cream
BOTTOM:	muffin	muffin
	fried egg	slice of cheese (B)
	onion slice	fried egg
	muffin	muffin
	sardines	scoop of Camembert (B)
	potato salad	cooked bacon, tomato
	muffin	muffin
	cucumbers	slice of beef
	smoky-cheese spread	slice of onion
	muffin	muffin spread with blue cheese
	Parmesan cheese	cooked bacon
	tuna in mayonnaise	peanut butter
	muffin	muffin
	canned pizza sauce (B)	jam
	onion slice	cream cheese
	muffin	muffin

cheese, cooked bacon (B)
chutney
muffin

Finally, in this department, a good curry-flavored spread.

It takes chopping, but it goes far and keeps well, covered in the refrigerator.

CURRIED MUFFINS

Mix together

1 cup chopped ripe olives	½ cup mayonnaise
½ cup thinly sliced green onion[1]	½ teaspoon salt
1½ cups shredded American cheese	½ teaspoon curry powder.

Spread it on a toasted muffin half and broil it till the cheese melts. This is equally good, of course, on any kind of toasted bread or split roll.

2. The Egg

If you automatically think Eggs when you're wondering what to eat, you should automatically think Big Eggs when you're at the grocer's. Little ones are no bargain, and I don't know why the hens bother to lay them. If a recipe calls for one egg, a small one can often spoil it. All the recipes written today assume that you're using large eggs.

The egg group is closely allied to the muffin group, as we have seen. Indeed, it is sometimes hard to say whether a dish is an egg on a muffin or a muffin under an egg.

Egg eaters have their comfortable habits, too: soft-boiled, hard-boiled, scrambled with diced ham or Spam. . . . And sometimes they branch out, putting a fried egg on a

round slice of fried corned beef hash
round slice of fried scrapple.

Or they spread anchovy paste on toast and put a poached egg on it. If they are quite rich, they buy Hollandaise to put on it. (They'd never make it.)

Another good egg arrangement is

WOLFE EGGS

(Which differ from chicken eggs in that they came out of a Nero Wolfe mystery story)

[1] To Easterners these are scallions, to Westerners green onions, so I will call them green onions.

Fry two pieces of bread on both sides in plenty of butter, then spread them with liver paté. (You could use potted ham, but it was liver paté in the book.) Either fry gently or poach two eggs, one for each slice of bread. Place them on the bread, sprinkle generously with Parmesan cheese, and slide them under the broiler for just a minute.

3. The Milk Shake

The very term Milk Shake implies that you have a blender,[2] which is devoutly to be hoped, when you hate to cook and live alone. Though you'll use it only for a milk shake and, at rare intervals, crumbs or soups, it is well worth having. When you are healthy, it saves you time and effort, and when you are sick, alone, it can practically save your life. When you have the flu, for example, a milk shake made with an egg and brandy can be edible or drinkable when little else is.

A big point about the milk shake is that it's hard to make a bad one. Though proportions are basically

    1 cup milk
    1 average scoop of ice cream
    2 tablespoons syrup or 1 teaspoon flavoring

you can vary them according to what you have. It will be thicker or thinner or fruitier or not so fruity but still good.

When you count heavily on milk shakes and haven't too much ice-cream storage space, vanilla is the best kind to keep on hand, because it combines well with so many things:

    frozen or canned fruit
    rum, brandy, whisky (or rum or brandy flavoring)
    instant coffee
    sliced bananas
    thawed frozen fruit-juice concentrates
    fruit, chocolate, or caramel syrups.

And that is only a start. Add sugar if it seems to need it, or an egg if you want extra nourishment.

4. The Soup

Soup devotees have an easy time of it. Usually they prefer

[2] Of which more in Chapter 4.

the frozen, then the dehydrated, and then the canned, in that order. Or they mix a couple of cans in the blender. But the selection all around is limitless, and they haven't a problem. With a roll or crackers, and fruit or a bakery fruit pie, they consider themselves fed.

5. The Baked Potato

People who depend subconsciously on baked potatoes usually depend, as well, on an aluminum nail to bake one quickly. This cuts the time in half, and the baking from inside out seems to improve the potato.

Then they butter, salt and pepper it and eat it.

For a special occasion, they might use it as a base for something else—creamed chipped beef or cheese sauce or canned chicken à la king or creamed canned tuna. But not often.

Or, in a burst of unprecedented kitchen activity, they can simmer 1/4 pound of fresh mushrooms in about 3 tablespoons of butter, add half a cupful of sour cream, simmer it till it's hot, and pour it over the split baked potato. With a tall glass of wine or vegetable juice, this is a good dinner.

"I had a marvelous dinner in a motel all by myself, that I cooked on a little stove. Three baked potatoes, sour cream, and a whole pound of caviar a friend sent me."
—TRUMAN CAPOTE

In addition to cleaving with fair consistency to one of the categories we just passed, the reluctant solo cook usually shows an unswerving loyalty to a small group of prepared pantry items, if they taste all right and are easy enough. Another person might start to twitch after the second night on Corn Chowder, with a probable third coming up. But not the people who hate to cook. It appeals to them—as Mt. Everest did to Mallory—because it is *there*.

Other things that can be steady and comforting friends, depending on your personal taste buds, are:

> canned corned beef hash with some Worcestershire and chopped onion added. Fry it crisp. If you have any Swiss or Cheddar, grate a little on top and let it melt under the broiler;

canned ravioli, with plenty of Parmesan;

chili. There are several good canned varieties to heat and serve plain or pour over the Classic Hamburger.

The list can go on and on, for everyone has favorites.

Another good pantry item to keep handy is dietetic tuna. Packed without oil, it's white, tender, and expensive, but it tastes very much like chicken.

And while we're touching ever so delicately on seafood, a good swift recipe is

OLD STONY-LONESOME'S SEAFOOD NEWBURG

½ cup canned cream sauce
½ cup crabmeat
¼ cup cooked shrimp

Heat the cream sauce, then add 2 teaspoons sherry and the seafood. Bake it in a casserole for twenty minutes at 350°, with crumbs on top if you have some.

The matter of vegetables

Getting enough vegetables is no problem if you like them. You munch raw carrots, turnips, celery, and so forth, and you don't mind making a meal of tiny canned French peas (drained and heated with lettuce and onion and butter).

But this happy attitude isn't shared by everyone. Like curly hair or a taste for opera, it's probably something you're born with. If you didn't happen to be, your solution is usually to throw out some old lettuce every couple of weeks (because you buy it even though you don't eat much of it, and it goes west with remarkable speed).

The average delicatessen isn't much help. Delicatessens usually specialize in the macaroni or potato or gelatin sort of salad, which isn't what you need. Also, you could buy half a dozen cabbages for the price of a pint of their coleslaw. (See, incidentally, page 64.)

In this situation, if you customarily eat lunch out, you can make lunchtime Garden Produce Time, at a place where the soups and salads are good.

For home consumption, you can look into the dehydrated salad dressings, which are usually better than the bottled. If it is a good strong-flavored one, like the Roquefort or the Caesar, you'll find you can taste hardly anything through it. You can also mix it with a package of the frozen mixed vegetables, cooked and chilled, and eat it till it's gone.

It is wise to keep big cans of vegetable juice around, and drink a glass now and again. Some brands taste quite all right, even without the vodka. If they don't, celery salt and Tobasco may help.

Another good approach to the vegetable is a can of concentrated beef consommé, chilled until it's jelled, then casually mixed with almost any salad vegetable or combination of them.

These could be

> coarsely chopped tomato
> coarsely chopped avocado
> coarsely chopped cucumber
> thinly sliced zucchini squash
> watercress or parsley.

Put it all in a chilled bowl, with a lemon wedge on the side.

This is a good breakfast on a hot morning, by the way, and it is also handy to remember as a first course for dinner, should you be feeding a guest. It gives the impression that you eat better than you do, and that they are eating more than they are. It is a good put-off—the old British boarding-house term for something that partially fills the stomach before the roast appears and thus makes the meat go farther.

The matter of desserts

Desserts are fruit, or a bakery cake—like applesauce cake, which keeps best—or a frozen cake, or a sack of chocolate bars, or *marrons glacés* over some ice cream (and it is marvelous how much longer the marrons last when there is only you to eat them). In other words, you never make desserts, you buy them.

I read an article once about cooking for one that gave directions for an easy one-person mousse. You whip ½ cup of whipping cream, add ½ cup of crushed strawberries, with a little sugar, then freeze for three hours. But the reluctant cook sees—with that swift grasp of essentials that distinguishes her every move—that it would have a basically strawberries-in-ice-cream taste, and be more work. She might just as well buy some French vanilla ice cream and pour the berries over it. Which is what she does.

The matter of shopping

Recently, a man I know wanted to buy a compact car. When he exclaimed over the high price of one, the salesman shrugged and said, "Well, if you want economy, you gotta pay for it."

This is truly the case when the solo cook buys groceries. Even so, the Tiny Extravagant is cheaper in the long run than the Large Economy. When you shrewdly buy five pounds of potatoes at a resounding bargain price, you bask in the glow of it for weeks, while the potatoes sprout quietly away. So it's best to buy small amounts of everything except possibly the canned or dehydrated stand-bys you know you'll eat.

Instant freeze-dried herbs and vegetables, which we'll consider further in Chapter 4, have taken away the institutional fragrance from the word "dehydrated."

And you should not forget about old-fashioned dried foods when you're cooking, or not cooking, for yourself. Powdered milk is good to keep handy as an ingredient, unless you drink so much fresh milk that you can depend on yourself to have it around. The powdered kind makes good milk shakes and milk punches, too.

Dried fruit is handy—more dependable than fresh, cheaper than frozen, and it has interesting possibilities. You can put plump dried prunes in a jar, cover them with gin, and leave them for a week. (Be sure they're the plump ones, for the hard wrinkled kind will just sit there squinting at you, no matter how much gin they're in.) These are good with after-dinner coffee.

Indeed, they open a rich field of research. You might try marinating apricots in brandy or bourbon, figs in tequila, dates in slivovitz. . . .

Frozen foods are fine, of course, though they're still not the entire answer. There is a limit to the number of TV dinners you can eat (and some people reach it with the first one.)[3]

Too, the fact that most frozen foods are packaged to serve

---

[3] Frozen individual chicken or meat pies are more satisfactory. I know a lady—and an accomplished cook she is—who adds sherry to a jar of chicken, creamed, and pours it over the tops of hot chicken pies, to hearten them a bit. This is a good solution for luncheon guests.

three or more creates problems. You could cook it all, then eat cooked leftovers, which is dreary. Or add some of them to a green salad or a canned beef stew, but that isn't likely. Or saw the frozen chunk into thirds, repackaging and labeling each with care.

But people aren't usually that conscientious. The chunk is probably put back in its box, the end casually tucked in. Presently, ice crystals form inside, at which point the item is hardly worth eating, even if you felt like it.

The best answer, I think, is to buy nothing from a feeling of duty (*I really should eat more carrots*) or economy (*I loathe Brussels sprouts but they're five boxes for a dollar*). Instead, buy only what you truly like, and eat all of it at once. A package of whole asparagus, if you like it, with cheese in some form (or the All-Around Crumb Topping, page 106) is a satisfactory meal. Or chow mein. Or Beans Amandine. Or any of many others.

This brings us to the cheerful matter of balancing a couple of days instead of a couple of meals, which is the pleasantest way to operate by yourself.

Preparing those Basic 7[4] daily—the Basic 7 as touted by the government, bless its heart—is an appalling thought if you're of the noncooking persuasion. You're not about to do it.

But you can come out the same door, approximately, by thinking big, in forty-eight hour chunks. If one day is mainly meat and vegetables and the next is mainly fruit, cheese, and bread, you eat more of fewer things at one time. Which means fewer leftovers and less all-around preparation.

Clearly, the reluctant cook cooking for herself alone tends toward *la basse cuisine* instead of *la haute*. Still, there are many ways to run a railroad, and this one has its advantages.

A minor point but still a plus, it gives scope to what Virginia Woolf called one's angularities—a possible predilection for apple pie and cheese for breakfast, or artichokes seven nights running, or dinner that's wholly shredded wheat. You

---

[4] 1. whole-grain cereal or bread
2. fats: butter, oil, et cetera
3. proteins: meat, fish, eggs, cheese
4. milk, one pint
5. a citrus fruit and another fruit
6. a leafy green or yellow vegetable
7. a sweet

simply go along, taking your own sweet way and your vitamin pills.

More important still, eating to stay alive saves time and usually money that can be applied to activities a little closer to the heart.

CHAPTER 2

Anticlimax, The Daily

30 ENTREES FOR THE SIMPLE-MINDED & THE PURE IN HEART

*"There is no lasting hope in violence,
only temporary relief from hopelessness."*
—KINGMAN BREWSTER, JR.

All days lead but to the kitchen, or so it often seems at 5:00 P.M. And there is an astonishing number of days in the average lifetime.

Thirty uninspired but dependable recipes[1] will see you through about three decades in the kitchen. But if you're going to be standing around out there for longer than that, you'll need another batch. This chapter, it is hoped, will provide them.

[1] The number in the first book.

These recipes have all been reluctantly tested, and somewhat more cheerfully approved, by women who hate to cook. They call for no mysterious ingredients, and measurements are as clearly stated as possible. No "add a wineglass of Chablis" sort of thing.

Also, they try to explain what to expect—for instance, how long, if there's any doubt, a process takes. Recipes that don't are disconcerting. (Like "Beat egg yolks till thick and lemon-colored." I've never noticed that my egg yolks change color enough to get excited about, and as for thick, they start out that way.)

Another thing: most of these recipes specify *covered* or *uncovered*. If they don't, it's because it doesn't matter. (By the way, it's good to remember the virtues of aluminum foil should you ever find yourself midstream in a recipe that demands covering and the pot you are using is lidless.)

Whether these recipes are completely free of land mines is of course—another matter. The human element is involved here, and you know how that can complicate things. For example, a cookbook writer can say in her directions for Clam Shortbread, "Add the contents of a 7-ounce can of clams" to some biscuit dough. Because she has made this little masterpiece so often herself, she doesn't think to say "Drain the clams first."

But we literal-minded recipe-followers will simply do as we're told, ending up with a thick clam soup, which disorganizes us badly.

While I've tried to circumvent disasters like this, I know they can happen.

How they taste

You will find an occasional clue, if it seems indicated, as to how something is going to taste. It is curious the way good ingredients can sometimes add up so bad (and vice versa), yet you can't make a hard-and-fast rule about it. That is, some recipes[2] run true to form and taste exactly as bad as you thought they would.

Then there's the fact that there's no accounting for taste buds. If you simply don't like saffron or rutabagas, no saffron or rutabaga recipe is going to taste really good. Along these

---

[2] Only last week I carefully prepared a creamed-corn-and-water-chestnut recipe that gave every promise of being a mess and fulfilled it nicely.

paths we must walk with tolerance, as we pad o
repertoires.

One more troubling thing for cookbook writers is
how many people a recipe will serve. Actually,
who knows? It depends on the people and the menu. So I've
pussy-footed by saying "servings," which means that four
servings could serve four people once or two people twice or
one high-school boy for an afternoon snack.

Only an occasional menu suggestion is given, by the way,
because menus so often tend to peter out. What sounds good
and even possible at nine in the morning often sounds like
more trouble than it's worth at blast-off time, or 5:30 P.M.

So we'll wade into it now, with the following reasonably
quick stand-by recipes, which taste good to us who make
them. Some of them involve protein plus a vegetable or a
starch, which eliminates cooking something else. They'll all
do what they are expected to do, the Lord willing and the
creek don't get up, and they're grouped according to the
main protein that's in them, starting with a small stampede
of beef recipes right here.

Perhaps you remember Sweep Steak, which calls for a 2-
to 3-pound pot roast with a package of dry onion-soup mix
sprinkled over it, the whole thing then sealed snugly in heavy
aluminum foil, placed in a pan (in case it springs a leak),
and baked at 300° for three hours or 200° for nine hours.[3]

It is my pleasure, at this time, to present

1. SWIPE STEAK

6-8 servings

which is the same thing except that you add a can of undiluted condensed mushroom soup *in addition to* the dry
onion-soup mix. All this adds up to good gravy when you
unwrap it.

Another interesting new development is

---

[3] Do this so that dinner will be ready if you're going to be away
from home all day.

2. SWOOP STEAK

6-8 *servings*

This time, put the round steak in a Dutch oven or a similar heavy iron skillet with a lid. Put the dry onion-soup mix on the meat, then pour 2 cups of Burgundy wine on top of it all, replace the lid, and cook it the same way.

With any of these three steak recipes, you can add potatoes, carrots, and celery—if you like, of course—for the last half hour, if you're cooking at 300°; for the last hour if you're cooking at 200°.

Now we'd better let that recipe rest. Either Sweep, Swipe, or Swoop will answer your modest pot-roast requirements, so let's not do anything else to it. There is an ever-present danger that enthusiastic cooks will take a recipe like this and fancy it up ("just throw in some fresh mushrooms, shallots, celery root, coriander, rosemary, oregano, basil, and seventeen artichoke hearts . . ."), and there goes your recipe.

3. HORSERADISH BRISKET

6-8 *servings*

(*This is good with or without the horseradish sauce, but the sauce is certainly easy.*)

Settle a 3- to 4-pound fresh boneless beef brisket in a pot with a lid. Then add

> enough water to cover the meat
> an onion cut in half
> a handful of celery tops or pieces
> salt and coarse-ground pepper.[4]

Put the lid on and simmer it three or four hours, or till it's tender.

Then, for the horseradish sauce: Add a tablespoon of lemon juice and horseradish—to taste—to a can of cream sauce (or a cup of cream sauce you make yourself). A little more pepper is good in the sauce, too.

---

[4] The kind that comes already coarse-ground in jars—sometimes called Java cracked—is handier for cooking and makes you sneeze just as hard.

With any of these first three recipes, by the way, it's a good idea to buy a slightly larger piece of meat than you'll need. Then the next night's dinner can be

4. POT-ROAST BUNS

4 servings

(Which are good and not much trouble)

Have 2 cups of beef bits and 4 hamburger buns ready.
For 20 minutes simmer together

2 tablespoons vinegar	a lemon slice
¾ cup water	a medium onion, sliced
1 teaspoon sugar	2 tablespoons butter.
2 teaspoons prepared mustard	

Then add ½ cup catsup or chili sauce and 1½ tablespoons of Worcestershire and the meat. Simmer it, covered, for forty-five minutes. Then spoon it out onto the toasted buns.

Ground beef is the basis of the following seven recipes, for the reason that when your intentions outshine your follow-through, you still have the hamburger there, ready to pan fry as usual, and no harm done.

However, each of the following seven has an additional point in its favor, and sometimes several. For instance, the next one is pretty, and uncomplicated, and tastes good with instant mashed potatoes.

5. ROSY MEATBALLS

4 servings

To a pound of ground beef, add

    ½ cup crumbs (packaged or homemade, see page 63)
    an egg
    1 teaspoon instant minced onion
    ¼ teaspoon dry mustard
    salt and pepper.

Shape them into Ping-Pong-size balls and brown them in butter, in something that has a lid.

Now mix an 8-ounce can of tomato sauce with a 1-pound can of whole cranberry sauce, to pour over the meatballs.

Do so, and simmer them, covered, for half an hour. Reheat them just before serving.

Another cheerfully variable ground-meat recipe is called Cornish Pasties if you are English, and if you are a Scotsman,

6. FORFAR BRIDIES

makes 4 servings that would take care of 2 people as an entree

a package of pastry mix

½ pound raw hamburger (or chopped leftover cooked or uncooked beef, veal, or lamb)

a small carrot, grated or diced

a small potato, diced

a medium onion, ditto, or 1 tablespoon minced onion

salt and pepper—not much

something to moisten it: 3 or 4 tablespoons of any soup or canned gravy or mushroom sauce; or ¼ cup bouillon, made with ½ cube or ½ teaspoon powdered

Roll out the pastry and cut four circles the size of salad plates. Mix everything else, put a dollop of it on each circle, fold your Bridies into half-moons, and seal the edges with a fork. Prick them, and bake at 400° for twenty-five minutes.

(If you brush them with egg white before you bake them, they'll have a shiny professional look.)

Those Bridies can be completely prepared ahead, right up to making them. Which brings us to an important truth, which should be hand-lettered on the boudoir wall as a constant reminder:

There's hardly a recipe that can't be interrupted at least three-quarters of the way along, with no ill effects, then finished shorly before dinner, AFTER YOU'VE REHEATED IT TO THE POINT WHERE YOU LEFT IT.

It is important to look at recipes in this light. To make it easier, I think I will put STOP HERE[5] in recipes where it makes

---

[5] I was going to use only the initials SH, but I found that it gave a strangely hushed and reverent feel to the page.

sense (which it doesn't if something takes only five minutes anyway).

What you do with it after you've stopped depends on what's in it and how long it will be before you start it again. I see no reason to refrigerate something entirely cooked (or a casserole that's mainly cooked meat, cooked rice, and cheese, for instance) if I'm going to reheat it in a few hours. I leave it on top of the stove. It's everyone's own decision, I think, and depends, too, on how full the refrigerator is.

And now we come to the matter of *when* to cook; for a valuable thing to know about cooking besides how to get out of it is when to get into it.

I wish I had learned earlier that for a girl who gets to the kitchen on reluctant feet, it is best to cook, whenever possible, at the more repellent times of the day. If those pastry circles in Recipe 6 had been cut out, say, at noon, the Forfar Bridies' chances of showing up for dinner would have improved immeasurably. Just which *are* the more repellent times of the day is, clearly, one's own decision.

I find that I am in general agreement with the old monastery maxim: "The morning is the Lord's and the evening is the angels' but the afternoon is the Devil's."

That is, I like to tend my own trade—writing—in the fresh morning hours 5:00 A.M. to noon, which is the time for a walk, lunch, and whatever else needs doing, till around 3:00. I wouldn't dream of spoiling an evening or a cocktail hour with cooking. So, midafternoon is my time to cook when I do, for I seldom can think of anything bright to do with midafternoons anyway.

If my office were elsewhere, or if I had very small children now, this wouldn't work. I'd have to think of something else. But I would still choose, to the extent that I could, whatever hour seemed most generally pointless. Hour is about it, too. It is astounding what you can do in an hour if you have to.

The next recipe—a domesticated version of a well-known San Francisco specialty—is good, fast, and highly expandable or retractable. Just add more eggs, or less spinach, or more hamburger.

7. CASUAL JOE'S SPECIAL

4 servings

some hamburger—½ to 1 pound
some chopped spinach—a package of frozen, cooked
    and drained; or a can of spinach, drained; or
    cooked drained chopped spinach, though that is
    a lot more trouble
some olive oil—say, 3 tablespoons
some onion or garlic—a cut garlic clove sizzled in
    the oil and then removed, or a teaspoon of
    minced onion, or half a chopped onion—what-
    ever you feel up to
some eggs—say, one per customer, beaten slightly
salt and pepper

Heat the olive oil in a skillet with the onion or the garlic.
Add the ground beef in small bits. Pan fry[6] it till it's as done
as you like it. Then add the spinach, STOP HERE, and stir it
around till it's hot. Then add the eggs and stir till they're
cooked. Salt and coarse-grind pepper it, and serve it.

If you like curry, this next one is handy to know. Most
curries seem to involve lamb, chicken, or fish, but this is how
you can

8. CURRY HAMBURGER

4 servings

In a skillet that has a lid, sauté a chopped onion in oil or
butter, then add

a pound of ground beef   1 teaspoon curry powder
salt and pepper   ¼ teaspoon garlic salt.

Stir it around till the meat is brown. Then add
            2 8-ounce cans of tomato sauce
            1 cup water.

[6] I'd rather say "fry," because I get tired of "sauté," and I think
I was happier before I knew "fry" means "deep-fat fry" as in
doughnuts. Now I feel duty-bound to say "pan fry" when I mean
"use a greased skillet," for fear someone will think I don't know
any better. Thus education doth make cowards of us all.

Simmer it covered for ten minutes. STOP HERE. Then, five minutes before dinnertime, add a squirt of lemon juice. Serve it on rice with whatever trimmings are available: chutney, sliced green onions, crumbled bacon . . .

The last three ground-beef affairs are Combinations or Casseroles, and it might be well to look hard at the casserole before we get into it.

Most men don't regard the casserole too highly. You seldom hear a man reply, if you're so foolish as to ask him what he'd like for dinner, "Why don't you make that good prune-chicken-broccoli whatchamacallit?"

If you retitle it a Stew or a Goulash, it stands a slightly better chance with him. Even so, he'd rather have a piece of meat, or, at any rate, a hamburger in recognizable form.

Remember, too, that a casserole is economical only when it's to serve a lot of people, or when it is creatively concocted out of odds and ends by a good cook who loves to. She also knows how to serve it with aplomb, but unfortunately this doesn't come in cans.

The rest of us wouldn't dare clean out the refrigerator for a casserole, or want to. We simply go buy the pimentos and all the other things the recipe demands. Which doubles or triples the cost of the ground beef we could have served plain.

Fatalistically, we realize when buying these things that it will probably be a long old time before we need pimentos (and the other things) again. So far as those pimentos are concerned, you can keep them healthy for a considerably longer time if you transfer them into a small glass jar and add a teaspoon of vinegar and cover them with water. But this probably won't get done; and so the rest of the pimentos will idle themselves into a hairy old age if you don't promptly throw them out.

Yet there are times, even in the life of the reluctant cook, when she feels an inner need to make a casserole. After she's tasted a good one somewhere else, perhaps. Or when she is in a rare nesting mood and the wind is right. A man is wise to let his wife have these occasional marabou moments, too. He probably isn't 100% perfect himself.

9. BOEUF AND OEUFPLANT

4 *servings*

(*What this is, actually, is good eggplant-and-hamburger sand-wiches baked in sauce. Presently, if you stay with it, you'll come to eggplant sandwiches without the boeuf, which will prove equally exciting in a different way.*)

  an eggplant, sliced in half-inch slices,[7] salted and peppered
  olive oil
  1 pound ground beef
  a jar of spaghetti sauce (1-pound size) preferably with
    mushrooms in it. If it has no mushrooms, add a jar of
    the broiled-in-butter kind
  ½ cup grated Parmesan or Romano cheese

In a little oil, pan fry the eggplant slices on both sides till they're light brown. Drain them on paper towels while you pan fry half as many hamburgers as you have eggplant slices. (You'll have to add more oil, because the eggplant really soaks it up.)

In a shallow casserole dish, layer the eggplant slices, with hamburgers between them. Cover it all with the sauce; top with the cheese. STOP HERE. Bake it, uncovered, for twenty minutes at 350°.

Finally, in the beef department, two Mexican-oriented dishes the first of which is quite good and the second of which children like. (Adults like it all right; they're just not writing home about it.) Both these recipes make good yard-age with a pound of ground beef.

10. PEON TORTILLA PIE

6-8 *servings*

In a little oil, sauté
    1 pound ground beef
    1 medium chopped onion

[7] You needn't peel it unless it's an elderly eggplant with horrid age spots and wrinkles. This would be one you bought some time ago and forgot about, because it would be foolish to start right out with an antique.

　　　　1 garlic clove, minced (or ½ teaspoon garlic p[...]
Then add
　　　　1 can condensed cream of chicken soup, undilu[...]
　　　　1 can condensed cream of celery soup, undiluted
　　　　½ can water
　　　　1 can green chili peppers, seeded,[8] rinsed, and diced.

Now cut in half 12 thawed frozen tortillas. Pour some of the beef mixture into a casserole, then add some tortilla halves, then more beef mixture, and so on, ending with the sauce. STOP HERE.

Bake it, covered, for an hour at 325°. Then top it with a cup of grated yellow cheese, and bake it, uncovered, another fifteen minutes.

11. TAMALE BEAN POT

　　　　6-8 servings as is, and easy to double or triple
(*You can bake this four hours at 200°, which would be handy on a football afternoon; or two hours at 350°, as you like it.*)

Brown 1 pound of ground beef with a minced garlic clove and 1½ teaspoon of chili powder. (If you like a more distinctly south-of-the-border taste, add another teaspoon.)
Then mix it with
　　　　1 can *garbanzo* beans, drained
　　　　2 cans red kidney beans, drained
　　　　1 can Mexicorn, drained
　　　　1 can tomato sauce
　　　　a spatter of Tabasco sauce
　　　　2 cans of tamales, papers peeled off,
　　　　　　and cut in 1-inch chunks.
Bake it, covered, either of the two ways mentioned above.

So endeth the beef section. And perhaps right here would be a good place for the eggplant affair mentioned earlier, which is not only beefless but wholly meatless, though it's a good hearty main dish.

[8] If you don't seed them they'll take the top of your head off. The seeds are *very* hot.

12. ARMENIAN SANDWICHES

3 servings as an entree, 6 as a vegetable accompaniment

Slice an eggplant in half-inch slices. Pan fry them a little in olive oil, and lay them out neatly on a paper towel.

Now pour half a beaten egg into a small bowl and add enough grated Parmesan or Romano cheese for a thick paste. Spread it on half the eggplant slices, and top them with the others.

Dip these sandwiches in the rest of the egg, then in some crumbs. STOP HERE. Pan fry them, both sides, in olive oil till they're a pretty light brown.

Now for a few PORK things.

13. THE PARSON'S HAM

2-3 servings

(*A good fast dinner when you've an eye on the clock and a foot in the flypaper*)

Cook ⅔ cup of rice.

Lightly pan fry a one-pound ham slice.

Put it on an oven-proof platter if you have one, and on a pan if you don't. Pile the rice on it, grate yellow cheese generously on top of the rice, and place it in a hot broiler for five minutes or so, till the cheese melts.

To round things out, you could arrange canned peach halves around it before you broil it, first putting a little brown sugar and butter into their hollows. But there isn't always time to round things out.

14. THE EASIEST RIBS[9]

4-6 servings

Allow a pound of spareribs per person, or ¾ pound of the small meatier back ribs.

[9] A virtually noncooking friend of mine, reading proof here, said, "But they're not as easy as roasting them plain at 500° for ten minutes and then 350° for an hour without any sauce at all, and mine are easier to eat." I couldn't think of a thing to say.

Mince or crush a garlic clove in a bowl and then add ¼ cup each of

> prepared mustard
> soy sauce
> bourbon
> brown sugar.

Add 1 teaspoon of grated orange rind, though this is not essential.

This will take care of 4 to 6 pounds of ribs. Spread it on both sides of the ribs and roast at 325° for two hours. Turn them once and baste them if you think of it.

Next comes a slightly different approach to pork chops.

Certainly, different doesn't always mean better. Recipes that boast like that always remind me—well, not always, but they did right then—of the inscription on the Scottish tombstone: "Lay down your burden and follow me." To which a shrewd passer-by had appended a neat sign:

> "To follow you I won't consent
> Until I know which way you went."

What is different about the next recipe is the soy sauce, which gives a slight Oriental aura to the chops, and some think it improves them.

15. APRICOT PORK CHOPS

6 servings

6 reasonably thick pork chops	2 tablespoons soy sauce
1 medium onion, finely chopped	a green pepper, thinly sliced, if you like it
1 medium can apricot halves	

Into a paper bag put a little flour, salt, pepper, and then the chops. Shake them firmly. Brown them in the fat you trimmed off, then add the apricots, onions, and soy sauce. Simmer it half an hour covered, STOP HERE, and half an hour uncovered. If you aim to add the green pepper, do it fifteen minutes before the chops are done.

If you occasionally cook a pork roast, the following dish will help use it up. (It's a good easy goulash anyway, made with 2 or 3 good-sized pork chops, boned, cubed, and browned.)

16. TOMORROW'S GOULASH

4 servings

Brown a small chopped onion in 2 tablespoons of bacon fat.

Add 1 tablespoon of paprika, and simmer it while you cube 2 or 3 cupfuls of the cooked pork.

Now add the pork, plus

>2 cups sauerkraut
>1 tablespoon caraway seeds.

Cover and simmer it for an hour. STOP HERE and reheat it when you're ready to serve. If it seems dry, add a little water. And just before dinnertime, stir in ½ cupful of yogurt.

17. OH DAD, POOR DAD
Or, Spam and Cheese

4-6 servings

(But if you don't tell him, he'll probably think this is ham.)

Grind up a can of Spam. Then mix it with

>2 beaten eggs
>20 2-inch-square soda crackers, crushed
>1 pint milk
>¾ cup grated sharp Cheddar,
>> plus a little more for the top.

Bake this, uncovered, in a casserole dish for an hour at 350°.

SEAFOOD will be the next consideration, with five recipes, the first being a well-bred little sole recipe.

Sole is an In fish, as you may have noticed. Many a cook depends on her little sole recipe as many another girl counts on her basic black. You might try counting on this one if you're not already committed. It's only a ten-minute operation—mixing a sauce, spreading it on the fish fillets, and rolling them up. But the results are rather impressive. And taste good.

18. RIVIERA SOLE

6 servings

Mix together
1 cup yogurt   1 tablespoon lemon juice
½ cup mayonnaise   ½ teaspoon curry powder.
    After you rinse 2 pounds of sole fillets, and pat them
dry with paper towels, spread half the mixture on them, salt
and pepper them, and roll them up. Put them in a shallow
buttered casserole and pour the rest of the sauce on.
    Over it all, sprinkle a can of drained broiled-in-butter
mushrooms and a can of drained white grapes. (Or you could
use raw mushrooms and fresh grapes. If you do, sauté the
mushrooms first in a little butter, then add the grapes and
cook two or three minutes more.)
    All this can be done at any time. Then bake at 350° for
half an hour.

19. BODDIAN SOLE

3-4 servings
(Not quite so well bred, but just as easy)
    You start with a pound of sole, or 4 large fillets. Lay them
out nicely in a baking dish.
    Mix

            1 can undiluted mushroom soup
            ½ cup cooked shrimp
            ½ cup white wine

and pour it over the fish. STOP HERE. Let it stand three hours,
and more wouldn't matter.
    Finally, sprinkle it with ¼ cup Parmesan cheese and bake
it, uncovered, for twenty minutes at 400°.

    A word about WINE, by the way, inasmuch as we just
passed some. There is a great deal of it around, and those
little old wine makers are understandably anxious that we
use it up.
    Sometimes their efforts remind you of the soap-selling
genius a while back who persuaded people to carve statues

ut of soap as well as wash with it. This got rid of a lot of soap. And after the recent spate of wine makers' recipe books and kitchen manuals, we mustn't be alarmed if they presently tell us to use a robust Burgundy to dampen the silage as well as the swordfish.

As it is, one finds some fairly improbable wine recipes. The wine makers like wine in cinnamon toast (you mix sugar, cinnamon, and butter into a paste with Marsala or sherry). Or wine on pork chops (bread them in dry biscuit mix, sauté them in butter, then simmer them in sherry). And they like wine in baked beans, in tuna salad. . . .

But not everyone does. Here you must keep a cool head, and taste it on your mind's tongue first. If it tastes good there, then try it. But be cautious about quantity. Here again, they like you to pour it on. There is a Let's-throw-away-the-chicken-and-drink-the-gravy School that it's best to steer clear of.

As to the grade of wine to use in cooking, there is disagreement. Some good cooks say, *Any* kind. Other good cooks say, Use the same wine in cooking that you'll serve later at the table. (I'll bet they don't always do it themselves, though, when it's a matter of a fine old vintage Bordeaux.)

The main consideration, it seems to me, should be the basic flavor—strong or slight—of the dish itself. Nuances are lost in a hearty beef stew that's redolent of onions and garlic. But a custard or a delicate fish or chicken is only as good as the wine is.

Now for a clam or two.

20. CORNELIA'S CLAMS

5-6 servings

(Cornelia sometimes adds chopped hard-boiled eggs to this. I think artichoke hearts would be even better.)

Drain 2 cans of minced clams, but save the juice.

Mix the clams, in the top of a double boiler, with
2 cans undiluted cream of celery soup
½ teaspoon Worcestershire sauce.

This is a little thick, so thin it a bit with the clam juice—just a few tablespoonfuls. A tablespoonful of sherry is good, too. Heat it till it's hot.

Serve it on something toasted, and decorate it with some chopped green onions or chives.

21. BOARDINGHOUSE CLAM HASH

6 *servings*

(*A clamelet plus potatoes, and easy, once you've solved the spuds. It takes four—cooked, peeled, and diced. You can do it yourself, cheaper, or reconstitute a package of instant hashed browns, faster.*)

    4 cooked potatoes, diced
    a medium onion, chopped
    4 tablespoons butter
    2 cans chopped clams, drained
    4 eggs beaten with 4 tablespoons cream (sweet or
        sour) and 4 tablespoons Parmesan

Pan fry the onions in the butter, then add the potatoes and plenty of salt and pepper. Cook it, uncovered, ten minutes. Once in a while, plow some of the brown crust back in. STOP HERE. Then put the clams on top, and over them pour the eggs-cream-and-cheese business. Cook it another ten minutes, uncovered, or till the eggs are set.

22. CUPBOARD CRAB COBBLER

4 *servings*

(*The purists may fault you for using canned crabmeat, but it can get you out of many a hole. The big point about this recipe is that it tastes good and its main ingredients come off the pantry shelf—the crab, the tomatoes, the cornbread mix.*)

Set the oven for 450°, then melt ¼ pound of butter in the top of a double boiler. Into it drop a half cup each of chopped green pepper[10] and onion, and cook till they're tender.

    Then blend in

½ cup flour	1 cup milk
1 teaspoon dry mustard	1 cup shredded Cheddar cheese
½ teaspoon Ac'cent (MSG)	

[10] It is in pantry-meal situations like this that the freeze-dried chopped peppers in jars are so helpful. See page 67.

and stir it all till it's really thick. Then add

>1 cup crabmeat (6½-ounce can)
>1½ cups drained tomatoes
>2 teaspoons Worcestershire sauce.

Pour it into a casserole, STOP HERE, then mix a package of cornbread mix according to the directions on the box. Pour it on top, and bake it, uncovered, at 450° for twenty minutes.

Several nice things have been happening to CHICKENS around the country while my back was turned. I'm glad to have this chance to pass them along. Neither one messes up a broiler the way broiled chicken does, or the ceiling, as fried chicken does.

The first is

23. INNOCENT CHICKEN

6 servings

(*If you follow the crumb suggestion on page 65, this will taste a bit different every time, but still innocent. There's no point trying to complicate it, either, with herbs or sauces, because many recipes are born complicated and this one wasn't.*)

You'll need

about 2 pounds chicken	3 cups crushed cereal (or crumbs)
pieces, fresh or thawed	½ teaspoon seasoning salt
¾ cup melted butter	salt and pepper.

Sprinkle the salt, pepper, and seasoning salt all over the pieces, dip them in the butter, then the crumbs, and lay them skin side up in a baking pan, STOP HERE. Bake, covered, for half an hour at 350°. Then baste it with the rest of the butter and bake it uncovered an hour longer at 250°.

The second, not quite so innocent but nearly, is

24. BASTARD BARBECUE

3-4 servings

(*You will probably be suspicious, as I was at first, of the brown sugar. But go ahead.*)

Salt and pepper and lavishly garlic-salt a cut-up fryer.

Put it in a shallow pan and sprinkle it generously with brown sugar (not the brownulated variety). Dot it with lots of butter and bake it, uncovered, about an hour, at 350°.

Then there is one other chicken event that belongs here. So that we won't become disorderly this early in the game, we'll number it

24A. BACHELOR'S CHICKEN MUNDAY

6-8 *servings*
(Just as easy, and with a good, interesting taste)

You need 2 cut-up frying chickens, or a similar amount of chicken breasts, thighs, and drumsticks. Put them in a casserole dish that has a lid.

Mix together

    ¾ cup catsup
    ½ cup mayonnaise
    3 tablespoons Durkee's Famous Dressing.

Now pour it over the chicken, put the lid on, and bake it from 1½ to 2 hours at 350°.

The next recipe is a bird of a different feather. It is here because it uses up leftovers the week following Thanksgiving. (Should you ever feel like making it from scratch, the easiest way to cook the chicken is on page 109.)

25. LEFTOVER FOWL SOUFFLÉ

6 *servings*

You need 3 cups of diced cooked turkey or chicken.

Sauté 4 green onions, chopped, in 2 tablespoons of butter. With the other hand, cook ⅓ cup of raw rice, which makes a cup of cooked. Or use enough Minute rice to make one cup.

Now combine

4 beaten eggs	4 slices bread, torn in small
1 can chicken broth	pieces
(standard 10-ounce can)	2 tablespoons chopped
1 small can condensed milk	parsley
	½ teaspoon herb seasoning.

To this reasonably damp mixture add the diced chicken, onions, rice, and a teaspoon of salt. Put it in a baking dish, cover it generously with grated sharp cheese, and bake it at 350° for forty-five minutes.

Next, a little lamb, which somehow straggled behind.

26. A GOOD THING TO DO WITH LAMB SHOULDER CHOPS OR LAMB STEAKS

For 4 chops or steaks, mix about ½ cup blue cheese with a few drops of Tabasco and a teaspoon of Worcestershire. Have this at the ready.

Rub the chops or steaks with a cut garlic clove and broil them, about 4 inches from the heat. If they are an inch and a half thick, broil ten minutes, a little less if they're thinner. Turn them over then, spread the cheese mixture on the up side, and broil them another five.

27. LAMALOHA LOAF

6-8 servings

(A good different meat loaf. When you slice it, don't be upset if it falls apart a bit, for that can happen to anyone. It does so because it's tender and two-layered.)

Mix all together

2 pounds ground lamb, lean as possible	½ cup chopped parsley
	2 eggs, unbeaten
1 cup cracker crumbs (that's 28 2-inch-square crackers)	2 or 3 tablespoons soy sauce
¼ teaspoon garlic powder (or 1 crushed garlic clove)	½ teaspoon salt, or seasoned salt
	½ teaspoon sugar
½ teaspoon cumin	½ cup catsup.

Divide this into two longish patties (so it will eventually add up to a loaf) and put one of them in a loaf pan. Down the middle, line up

an 8-ounce can of drained browned-in-butter mushrooms.

Along the sides, arrange

½ small can of pineapple tidbits.

Cover it with the second long patty. Seal the edges now and spread some catsup over the top. STOP HERE. Then bake for one hour and forty-five minutes at 350°. (This is longer than a beef loaf would take because most people like the lamb more well done.)

28. SHOULDER BAGS

Cut aluminum foil in 10-inch-square pieces.
On each, place

a salted-and-peppered lamb	a slice each of onion
shoulder chop	green pepper
an eggplant slice	tomato.

Pour a tablespoon of sherry on top, wrap them up swiftly (so the sherry doesn't run out) and snugly, then put them in a baking ban. Bake them an hour at 350°.

These are good with any sort of rice or pilaf.

29. LAMB AND LEMON

4 *servings*

(*An unexpectedly good flavor combination, and a nice change from garlic.*)

¼ cup olive oil
juice of a lemon (¼ cup)
1 teaspoon grated lemon rind.

Brush 8 1-inch-thick loin or rib chops with this, and broil them about 4 inches from the heat, seven to ten minutes on the first side, depending on how pink you like your lamb. Brush them occasionally as they broil and after you turn them over. Give them about six minutes on the second side. You may garnish each chop with a lemon slice if you have another lemon.

30. BIG STUFFED MACARONIS

4 *servings*

(*Manicotti noodles is the technical name for what this recipe was built around. But there are 17,000 different shapes of pasta, each called something different. What you want is BIG hollow noodles, big enough so that two of them, stuffed, are enough for a serving. And note carefully: you stuff these uncooked, which is easy. Stuffing a limp noodle is a job that shouldn't happen to anyone.*)

Mix together and stuff 8 noodles with

½ pound diced mozzarella or jack cheese	2 tablespoons grated Parmesan or Romano
½ cup cottage cheese	2 tablespoons soft butter
2 slightly beaten eggs	½ teaspoon each salt and pepper.

Lay them in a flat pan and cover them with a sauce of 1 package French's dried spaghetti-sauce mix made according to its directions with 1 can of tomato sauce.

Sprinkle with more Parmesan or Romano now, and cover the pan. STOP HERE. Bake at 350° for forty-five minutes.

These should do it, then, for the next three decades. But before we leave the kitchen for the supermarket, in the following chapter, just a word here on the important matter of

Keeping a stiff upper lip

When you hate to cook, another ailment you probably suffer from, besides apathy, is the inability to judge correctly your own work.

In those low moments, should the whole dinner taste a little seedy, you must remember that it probably doesn't to other people. You had a better chance than they did to get tired of the ingredients.

Neither is the meal quite so glorious as you may think in those rare euphoric moments when the soufflé soars and the salad dressing sings. (Remember, you're exceptionally fond of anchovies.) The truth usually lurks somewhere in the middle.

It can also help if you will scrutinize critically an occasional restaurant meal. Then, after you've eaten a slice of tired salami with a pickled mushroom—which passed for antipasto—plus a cardboard cutlet, a too-vinegary salad, and grocery-store ice cream that called itself Spumoni, ask yourself if you could unblushingly have charged $5.50 for that.

As a last resort, should these things fail you, you may turn to Dr. Bryan's truly astonishing words of aid and comfort on page 89.

CHAPTER 3

Attack, Counter

PADDLING THROUGH THE COMBAT ZONE

"Take it one more round."
—ROD MCKUEN

When you hate to cook, you mustn't blame yourself too much for getting gypped at the grocery store more often than most people do. You must remind yourself that there are other areas in which you are more canny, and try to think what they are.

The fact is, eating well but cheaply is a luxury you're not prepared to pay for, in terms of either time or attention—a fuzzy-minded attitude you probably inherited from some fuzzy-minded ancestors. (Unfortunately, one must choose one's ancestors when one is hardly old enough to choose anything very intelligently.)

Also, there is no real cure for your basic impatience with comparison shopping and slide-rule shopping, both of which should be done in order to get the most out of food money.

Now certainly you ought to buy the weekend and mid-week advertised Specials—first making sure they *are* specials[1] —at several stores, if several stores are nearby.

But so often the Special is corned beef, when you just finished some. Or paper towels, which you bought a dozen of yesterday, in an excess of domestic zeal, and you haven't room for any more. Even if you did, you don't feel like spending another cent right now on paper towels.

As for shopping with a slide rule, it's just about necessary, in this wide wicked country, unless you can tell instantaneously whether 25 cookies for 32¢ is cheaper than 35 cookies for 43¢[2] or whether a 13¼-ounce package of cookies for 43¢ is a better buy than a pound of cookies for 59¢.[3]

It is comforting to know that matters like this—as well as the Giant Family Cooky Pak, the Jumbo Economy Cooky Box, and so on—are a worry to the government, too. So they're working on it. Some day we'll have standard, clearly labeled packages, for though the mills of the government grind slowly, they grind exceeding small.

Until then, reluctant cooks (and therefore reluctant shoppers) would rather pay the extra few cents for the cookies than figure it out. Also, they sometimes feel: If it matters that much to you, you shouldn't be buying cookies anyway.

In this chapter, therefore, we'll try to stay out of the foggier areas.

Several truths shine bright as the major planets, such as the fact that a plastic lemon costs astronomically more per squirt than a bottle of reconstituted lemon juice. Nearly anyone can remember this and switch to bottled goods, unless he owns a plastic-lemon factory.

And let's look at some other facts, equally unarguable:

One 5-pound chicken is a better buy than two 2½-pound chickens, because of the more favorable meat-to-bone ratio.

Powdered milk is only 9 cents a quart and works fine in your cooking. It makes a good frothy milk punch, too—milk, egg, sugar, whisky, beaten with an electric mixer.

Instant coffee costs least to drink. If you don't like it, reg-

---

[1] Because sometimes an exciting advertised Special isn't specially priced, it's only advertised because the food packer paid for the ad.
[2] It is.   [3] It isn't.**   ** I think.

ular coffee is next cheapest if you make it in one-cup drip coffee-makers, one per customer. Most housewares departments have them. This way people aren't drinking coffee just to drain the pot.

The grocer's or supermarket's own brand of food (or grog) is usually good, and usually cheaper than most nationally advertised brands. I think it often comes out of the same pot (or vat).

Fresh strawberry time[4] is the best time to eat frozen strawberries, or at any rate to buy them. Prices are often cut then, to make room for the new season's pack.

If you catch them soon enough, you can teach puppies and kittens to like dry dogfood and dry catfood, both cheaper than the wet by quite a distance.

Small packages of anything usually cost more than large ones per ounce of food. And most things come a bit cheaper by the case.

But right here we run head on into a real problem of anyone who hates to cook. I refer to those occasional will-o'-the-wisp compulsions to act housewifely—*i.e.*, take advantage of Good Buys. And this can lead to a freezer compartment full of okra or a pantryful of clams that you never feel like cooking. (These housewifely compulsions generally melt away the minute you get the Good Buys home.)

Point One, therefore, is to buy in quantity only what you like (as we saw in Chapter 1) and automatically use, most of the time. I mean staples, like catsup and coffee, not Fringe Foods like okra and clams.

Of course, these are personal matters, and one man's Fringe Food is another man's staple. But whatever your Fringe Foods are, if you buy them in quantity they'll probably prove to be an extravagance without being any fun, and that's the worst kind.

Point Two, closely related, is to have some general notion of how long things keep.

Canned and frozen foods are regarded by most of us as immortal, although they are not. Chances are very good that you will outlive them, because you'll get tired of looking at them. Presently you won't see them any more, and there they'll sit.

---

[4] Or fresh asparagus time or bean time and so on.

On the whole, canned food has better staying power than frozen. If they are good sound cans, no dents or leaks, and if you keep them at about 70°, they will be good for about three years.[5] This assumes, however, that you got them newly hatched, when in reality they might have been on the grocer's or wholesaler's shelves for months. That's something to consider.

To keep frozen foods their maximum length of time, you need a fine rapport between your own freezer and the grocer's. Each should be at 0°. You can check your own with a freezer thermometer, and if it's wrong, ask a repairman what to do. But you can't always see the grocer's thermometer, and he won't always tell you. If these things matter greatly to you, you may have to change grocers, though my own tendency is not to worry too much over a degree or two among friends.

Assuming, then, that the temperature situation is well in hand, it might be well to look at some facts[6] about storing things, on the chance that a few will stick.

These frozen foods won't necessarily poison you after the time limit, though the fish might, but they won't taste very good.

(This is an incomplete list if I've ever seen one, and I'm sure I have. But you can get the whole story in a plain franked envelope by writing to your congressman.)

FROZEN FOODS YOU'D BETTER EAT WITHIN 12 MONTHS
    Raw beef steak
    Raw beef roast
    Raw lamb roast
    Raw whole chickens
    Cooked chicken and turkey pies
    Concentrated fruit juices: orange, apple, grape
    Cherries
    Peaches
    Raspberries
    Strawberries
    Fruitcake

FROZEN FOODS YOU'D BETTER EAT WITHIN 8 MONTHS
    Raw pork roast
    Raw veal roast

[5] Though pickles and sauerkraut may die in a year.

[6] From the U.S. Agricultural Research Service, as given in *$$$ and Sense* by Ella Gale, Fleet Publishing Corp., 1965.

Green beans
Green peas
Peach pie

FROZEN FOODS YOU'D BETTER EAT WITHIN 6 MONTHS
Veal cutlets and chops
Cut-up chickens and turkeys
Whole ducks and geese
Whole turkeys
Cooked turkey dinners
Pound cake
Yellow cake

FROZEN FOODS YOU'D BETTER EAT WITHIN 4 MONTHS
Lamb patties
Halibut, pollack, drawn whiting
Shrimp
Chocolate layer cake

FROZEN FOODS YOU'D BETTER EAT WITHIN 2 OR 3
MONTHS
Cured pork sausage
Bacon
Hamburger
Chipped steaks
Shucked clams
Tuna pies
White bread and rolls[7]

Clearly, it would be smart to date the frozen foods the minute they come home, but one seldom does.

Then there's the matter of mixes.

When you buy something ready-mixed or prepared, you're buying labor, of course, which is why it costs more. It is often a good bargain, too, if you like the product.

For example, prepared Noodles Romanoff that serves 4 costs—at this writing—49¢. To make it yourself takes some time and eight ounces each of

[7] And when you take them out of the freezer, they keep better in the refrigerator than in the breadbox, which is a good place for bananas, or old cookbooks, or car keys.

noodles	.33
cream cheese	.39
sour cream	.31

$1.03

plus a smattering of chopped onion, Worcestershire sauce, garlic, Tabasco, and crumbs—about .07, or $1.10 in all. The recipe serves four or five. You'd have four ounces of noodles left over, but that's about your only bonus.

On the other hand, it seems silly to buy the seasoned flour you shake and bake your chicken in. And some producers of totally prepared foods—such as broccoli in lemon-butter sauce—seem to value that sauce inordinately. It isn't much trouble to apply a little butter and lemon juice yourself, to plain cooked broccoli, and save a dime.

Or, when you buy breaded fish—and breading fish is easy to do—you may be buying about as much bread as fish. And it isn't very hard to add raisins to cereal or water to your own pancake flour, and it's usually cheaper.

Next, we come to the matter of premiums and trading stamps.

Some people enjoy getting anything short of a poke in the eye if they get it for nothing, or think they do. And—few things being free in this world—if it pleases you to think you found one, there's certainly no reason to pass it up.

For instance, if all you were looking for was a dry mop to rearrange the dust with, and you find one as cheap as the rest that's attached to an ABSOLUTELY FREE inferior plastic alarm clock, this is a little bonus. So you might as well take it along, because some days you don't want to get up anyway.

But one should be careful not to let the tail wag the dog, not to get a mop solely because an inferior flashlight comes with it, or a jar of jelly just because it's in one of those dandy reusable containers. I have a friend whose breakfast table is beginning to look like something out of Libbey sired by Du Pont, but she can't seem to stop.

Trading stamps are closely related. There is a heart-warming element about them, which trading-stamp detractors tend to minimize.

It is curious, in fact, how emotional one can become over trading stamps. Once, some friends and I decided to give another friend, for her birthday, a filled-up trading-stamp book each. It was like parting with an arm. One has lived with those stamps so intimately (it usually takes a while to get them out of the handbag and into the book), and they represent time and care, as well as considerable spit. We never did that again, I can tell you.

The fact is, while prices are generally a bit higher in trading-stamp places, still you feel you've something to show for your money besides food, which is so impermanent. Moreover, that $3.00-or-thereabouts stamp book can't disappear, as an ordinary $3.00 would, into the children's dentist or the plumber. It absolutely *must* be spent on something you want.

Therefore, it's a pleasant little hobby and no harm done if you want something in the trading-stamp catalog, and rather expensive if you don't.

Things to beware of

I believe the Irritation Quotient, or I.Q., of the reluctant cook is higher than most people's, and this can lead to unnecessary trouble.

For instance, from a standing start, she can get sicker quicker than most people do hearing a little jingle like "Nothing says lovin' like something from the oven." Or when an ad tries to sell her Sex when all she wants, at the moment, is Orange Juice, she'll sometimes make a violent mental note never to buy that brand.

However, this can be cutting off her own nose. The product may be perfectly all right, and even a good buy. It is the advertising agency, usually, and not the manufacturer that puts the Freud into the food. The manufacturers go along with it because they are basically good simple food people who are overly impressed by Madison Avenue.

So you must shut your eyes and often your ears to these things and simply consider the taste, the size, and the price.

Then there is the matter of the new package. Sometimes you'd rather like to know why the manufacturer changed the old one. Did the other fellows change theirs, and he's only following suit? Or did he, perhaps, put a thicker bottom on the bottle so that it holds only 6 ounces now instead of 7½, though it's priced the same?

(In a recent congressional hearing, a food packer explained, in some of the most enchantingly backside-to reasoning since Alice in Wonderland, that he lessened the quantity so that the customer wouldn't have to pay a higher price.)

When something like this comes to your attention, you can register a negative vote by buying something else. It probably won't change anything immediately, but it will make you feel better.

There is also the heavy thumb gambit. Sometimes you might try making an informal check, yourself, to see whether the presacked ten pounds of potatoes weighs ten pounds or nine and a half.

And the check-out counter presents pitfalls. Grocers used to train their clerks to put the fresh tomatoes in the bottom of the sack, then drop in the canned pumpkin from a considerable height.

They don't do this so much any more. But now some grocers, the rascals, teach the help to throw in the price of an extra item once in a while on a long list where it probably won't be noticed. If it *is* noticed, it's an Oops, sorry about that. (When you read about the handsome sums grocers lose annually to shoplifters, you marvel that more grocers don't do it. Still, we teach our children that they mustn't cheat just because Johnny does.)

In any case, it's a good idea for the customer to count purchases, periodically, and even total them herself if she can add that far. Not often, just once in a while. This will help keep the boys on the straight-and-narrow, and the customer solvent.

Speaking of lists, supermarkets rather count on your not making one, for few people do, in this day of the impulse buy.

Preoccupied cooks are exceptionally listless and therefore impulse prone. They face an additional hazard—that of buying something twice or three times. I once ended up with three little jars of fenugreek—I needed some for a recipe I was supposed to try but kept postponing. Each time I'd make a new resolve to try the recipe, I'd buy another jar of it, because I knew I wasn't the sort of person who kept exotic things like fenugreek around the house.

It's a good idea, therefore, for the person who hates to cook to stand and stare at her own food shelves and spice cupboard now and then, to make sure of what she has or hasn't.

Though she'll probably never be a list-maker, she may find the following Mental Crutch helpful for making a list in her head as she drives or strolls along:

One—Run	Three—Tree
Two—Zoo	Four—Door

Five—Alive	Thirteen—Hurting
Six—Stick	Fourteen—Courting
Seven—Heaven	Fifteen—Lifting
Eight—Gate	Sixteen—Licking
Nine—Wine	Seventeen—Leavening
Ten—Den	Eighteen—Waiting
Eleven—Football team	Nineteen—Pining
Twelve—Delve	Twenty—Horn of Plenty

Assume, then, that you need (1) Butter (2) Baking Chocolate (3) Nutmeg. . . . You tie Run vividly to Butter in your mind: you're splashing through yellow puddles of it, running over tall buttery mountains. Then, when you want to remember the first thing on your list, you think One, and your mind steps neatly from One to Run to Butter. Or it should. And so you proceed, chocolate-coating the animals at the zoo, and so on through twenty, if you like, and lots of luck.

I've stressed the list here because—mental or written—it is still the main weapon in the customer's small armory. And heaven knows we need something. It's unsettling to find you've spent the price of a good record or a new shirt on food you didn't know you needed till you saw it. (The unwilling cook would rather run amok in a clothes shop or a bookstore than a grocery.)

Yet never have products looked so appealing, nor food people found us so embarrassingly predictable.

For instance, they know we hate to stoop. They've found that we're twice as apt to reach for things at see level as we are at knee level.

They know we'll often buy four of something marked four for a dollar, when we wouldn't buy it individually for 25 cents.

They've learned that we flock, as sheep to the salt lick, when they heap things high and cluttered somewhere, without reducing the price of the items at all.

They've found also—and this surprised me—that quantities of things appeal to us far more than one or two. That is, if there are fifty identical cans of Jean's Beans on the shelf, we don't say to ourselves, "My there's a lot of Jean's Beans left—I guess nobody likes them very much." No, we reach for a couple. But if there are only two cans of Jean's Beans there, we will probably reach for something else.

It is interesting to ponder why we react like this, or anyway you might get ten seconds or so out of it, on a dull morning.

CHAPTER 4

Discoveries, Assorted Newish

BEING NOT THE LAST BY WHOM THE OLD IS TRIED

"On The Runway Of Life You Never Know What's Coming Off Next."
—ARTHUR KOPIT

Once upon a time, a lady was gifted with a piece of electrical equipment that could have been a Chinese noodle machine or a 120-volt pretzel-bender or an electroplated futuristic sock dryer, she couldn't tell which. As she was making glad cries and wondering, her little boy said, with resoluteness, "It'll be a good place to hide Easter eggs."

He showed the proper attitude here. It is important to think positively when we can.

But sometimes there isn't a positive side. Only the other

day, I saw that they have perfected an electric paper-towel-snatcher, designed to save us all from the arduous work of tearing off the paper towels by hand, which makes you wonder whither we're drifting, besides in the direction of a fat-wristed society.

Clearly, new kitchen equipment poses a problem for people who hate to cook. We're either reluctant to spend a cent on that end of the house or we're subject to short-lived but expensive spasms of buying a new gadget in the wistful hope that it will solve everything.

But we've learned that nothing does. We've learned that so many things don't work for us the way they work for the demonstrator.[1] We've learned, too, that some things are designed with a certain malevolence to take ten seconds off the preparation time and add ten minutes to the wash-up time, which is no bargain.

And yet, some things there be—gadgets, habits, food products, even attitudes—that can take some of the pain out of the kitchen.

First, there is the matter of equipment.

The importance of pairs and trios and even sextuplets

It didn't take me long in my kitchen career—say, five minutes—to realize that I needed another oven or roaster or *something*.

Indeed, as Eve discovered when she made her first apple-sauce cake, it required a temperature different from the ass's-jawbone casserole she wanted to bake at the same time. All right, she should have thought of this earlier and baked her cake in the morning. But she didn't.

When you hate to cook but have to, an additional baking and/or roasting appliance is almost essential, because it helps to compensate for inferior planning and forgetful shopping. When you have one and you've forgotten to buy the rice that was supposed to heavy up the chicken casserole, you're in a position to shift gears—broil the chicken in one oven, and bake the ready-mix orange muffins or whatever you have in the other.

An appallingly large variety of ovens is available, ranging from expensive ones that include rotisseries to simple camp

[1] Did you ever get involved with a bean Frencher?

types. Whichever kind you get doesn't matter, so long as it is easy to clean. And operate. With most of us, in the kitchen a little science goes a long way.

"My attitude towards the news that a body falling freely in a vacuum accelerates at the rate of thirty-two feet per second, or whatever the hell it is, has since childhood been 'Who cares?'"

———NORMAN WARD

Then, take the small cheap items, like measuring spoons. If you have a dishwasher, four or five sets of measuring spoons are a great help. Just use them up, dropping them into the dishwasher as you go. (One set, at least, should be the long-handled rectangular-bowled type, for reaching to the bottom of narrow jars.)

And measuring cups. Six aren't too many, ranging from the ¼-cup size to the quart.

Another thing: you owe it to yourself to buy enough frozen pies and somehow dispose of the contents so that you have a tidy collection of aluminum-foil pie tins. These, besides stacking neatly, have a curious psychological value. If you're reheating food, or if you sometimes feel compelled to muss some crumbs around in melted butter (see page 106 for why you might be), an aluminum-foil pie tin is a good thing to do it in. It feels so here-today-gone-tomorrow that you've no hesitation about throwing it out instead of washing it. Even if you don't throw it out, it was nice knowing that you could have.

Another item of kitchen equipment that can make life pleasant back there is a mirror and vanity shelf. Kitchen designers put miles of shelves inside cupboard doors for you to fill with spice jars. There is no reason you can't use one for a mirror and make-up. Then when you're feeling warm and ratty around the edges like a bride's poached egg, you can do something about it on the premises.

A point about pots

Unfortunately, a pot—stew pot, saucepan, double boiler, whatever it is—had better be a good pot if it is in the kitchen of someone who hates to cook. Otherwise it won't last very long. Its bottom will burn out as it sits empty on the red-hot burner. Heavy cast-iron skillets and Dutch ovens are usually preferable.

They're even better for you. As Dr. Carl V. Moore, authority on anemia, recently told a medical-association meeting, "Food cooked in this type of utensil has a much higher iron content, and the gradual substitution of aluminum and stainless steel for iron in the manufacture of cooking utensils may have a most unfortunate effect on dietary iron intake." [2]

He noted further that studies of the iron intake of populations all over the world show that the large amount of iron consumed by the Bantus of Africa is due to their custom of cooking food and fermenting beverages in iron pots.

It might be said, of course, that all that iron hasn't got the Bantus very far. But be that as it may. What mainly concerns us is the fact that when your whole attention isn't on your cooking, you need all the help you can get. A flimsy pot gives you very little, and it increases, immeasurably, your chances of disaster.

Additionally, when you specialize in interrupted cooking, observing some of the STOP HERES in the recipes throughout this book, the cast-iron things plus porcelain-coated pots or casseroles make considerable sense. You can reheat the food on the stove burner, to the point where it was when you left it, then finish it in the oven.

As to smaller gadgets, anyone who doesn't have a separate minute-minder yet will produce fewer charred cookies after she gets one. It's always the last batch that is cremated.

Another thing: I found that my poached-egg performance improved immeasurably when I got a poacher. But my English muffin slicer hasn't changed my life any, though I know a lady who would rescue hers first if her house caught fire.

As to the little gourmet gadgets, they, too, are a highly individual matter. One girl's Mouli[3] is another girl's mistake. Though it is a great little garnisher, it takes an interminable time to grate or mince sizable quantities of anything. If you are nicely adjusted to a grater for cheese and kitchen shears

---

[2] As quoted in *The Women's Medical News Service*, 1965.

[3] I mean the little French rotary mincers for fresh herbs, and rotary graters for crumbs, cheese, and so forth. They're about a dollar in most kitchenware departments, or at the Bazar Français, 666 Sixth Ave., New York, N. Y.

for parsley, you probably won't acquire the Mouli habit. Habit has a great deal to do with these things.

The French garlic press has its fan club. But I find it almost magically hard to clean. Moreover, if it isn't cleaned immediately, the whole kitchen smells like a low-grade pizza parlor. More and more often I use garlic powder. Not garlic salt. Garlic powder. (When it's a matter of only peeling a garlic clove, swat it hard with the flat side of a heavy knife.)

My brief encounter with the French salad basket was also unrewarding. I mean the collapsible kind you swing around at arm's length to dry the greens without bruising them. It was raining that night, so I used it in the kitchen, and a couple of guests thought it was raining indoors, too. And I didn't think it really dried the greenery.

(When I feel like doing it right, I wash the greenery in a sinkful of cold water, separate it, lay it on a fresh dish towel, wrap it up like a tramp's bindle, and pat it or swing it dry. Then I wrap it in paper towels and put it in a plastic bag. But most of the time, I just wash it, drain it, and put it in the hydrator, and five minutes later it's sitting in a puddle of water.)

And so it goes; each to her own. Good pots and good knives, well sharpened, seem the main essentials for the person who hates to cook—and oddly enough, for the person who likes to. The best cooks I know go along cooking with whatever they have, unless something comes along that makes truly revolutionary sense. They don't upgrade their equipment from year to year, as the merchants of discontent would have us do.

Indeed, one sometimes wonders. Last year's whatever-it-is was heralded as The Ultimate. But this year's brand-new Ultimate makes last year's look sick. You get the impression that the manufacturers and ad men are backing away from it, daintily holding up their trouser legs and scraping their boots, the way a city slicker leaves the barnyard.

Still, that old Ultimate has served you all right, even though it doesn't have a Contour Handle. So take a deep breath and relax. There will be another Ultimate next year.

As for electrical appliances, they should be studied carefully before they're bought. One must try to visualize how they'll fit into one's own system—to use the word loosely— of running a kitchen.

Should you decide on an electrical gadget as fundamental as a can opener, do not—in an excess of enthusiasm— throw the old hand-operated variety away. In out-of-the-way places such as Bolinas (pop. 320) and in-the-way places like New York City (pop. 7,781,984), the power sometimes goes off.

And now, before we move on to some possibly helpful habits and some new groceries, let's stop for a short visit with

The blender

For years I thought—foolishly, as it turned out—that a blender was something that liquefied turnips and was hard to clean. Then I was given a blender, by a lady who owned two.

It is probably one of the earlier models. Undoubtedly some refinements have been added, though my basic lethargy in the field has prevented me from finding out. Anyway, I wouldn't look a gift blender in the bowl except when I'm washing it, which couldn't be easier,[4] and it hasn't liquefied a turnip yet.

What it *has* done, among other things, is improve the weekend lunch situation. Little children like to make their own milk shakes, which I consider a superb idea if they'll clean up after themselves. Even a man who isn't especially milk-shake prone often likes one made with a shot of bourbon, and he usually won't mind fixing it himself. You can suggest that he drop an egg into it, too.

As for recipes, a blender doesn't exactly fix you up pronto with a "dazzling array of epicurean delights," as the box around mine said. Indeed, one must beware of enthusiasts who call something "Blender Beef Stew" when it contains eighteen ingredients, only two of which ever see the blender. Thus you can be hoodwinked into trying a recipe that—like a built-in set of bunk beds—sounds like a practical idea but is a real pain in the neck to make.

But it does greatly simplify some recipes you wouldn't ordinarily bother with. Some of these are scattered throughout this book, and a few of them are right here.

For instance:

---

[4] Certain situations like fruit pulp may call for a bottle brush, but it's nothing serious.

BLENDER COLESLAW

The idea is this:

You fill ⅔ of the blender with chunked vegetables—cabbage, green or white onions, carrots—then add water up to the top. Flick the switch on and off several times. Drain it well in a sieve and repeat till all the vegetables are chopped.

Proportions for 4 servings would be

½ medium cabbage	4 green onions
1 small carrot	¼ green pepper.

For a dressing, mix

½ cup sour cream	1 or 2 teaspoons sugar
¼ cup mayonnaise	salt
2 tablespoons vinegar	pepper.

The chipped beef situation

The central fact about chipped beef is that few men with military or naval backgrounds regard it with any enthusiasm. But women buy it because it keeps so well. It's like money in the bank, that ever-ready jar of chipped beef, waiting on the shelf. Which it continues to do, because so few men will eat it.

The following blender-made spread makes a good sandwich, especially on pumpernickel or dark rye. With frozen vegetable soup or frozen green pea with ham, you could call it supper. And it generally fools the lads and uses up the chipped beef.

GOOD BEEF SPREAD

In the blender put

2 teaspoons onion flakes	1½ tablespoons mayonnaise
2 chopped hard-boiled eggs	½ teaspoon prepared mustard
¼ cup chopped celery	½ teaspoon lemon juice.

6 or 8 stuffed green olives or a pimento

Flick the switch on for six seconds or so. Then chop—because a blender won't really grind [5]—the contents of a 5-ounce jar of chipped beef, mix it all thoroughly, and spread it on the pumpernickel.

[5] My blender booklet didn't say what it *wouldn't* do. So I learned, myself, that it won't whip eggs, or mash potatoes, or crush ice, or grind meat.

Before the chipped beef gets entirely away from us, it might be well to point out that ordinary creamed chipped beef is twice as good if you give it a shot of cognac.

One final word before we sail away from the blender and into something else. It is fact, sterling and indisputable, that a blender swiftly

> grinds coffee beans
>
> makes bread crumbs, both fresh and dry. (A leftover dinner roll or French bread—even buttered and garlicked—makes good crumbs, too, though if the bread's been buttered, be sure you refrigerate the crumb jar.)
>
> de-lumps hardened brown sugar
>
> makes remarkably good soups from quite ordinary ingredients—just check the blender booklet
>
> crushes crackers for piecrusts or casserole toppings (and it will similarly take care of the last third of a box of cereal the family lost interest in. To that, you can add the last six soda crackers or tired cheese crackers or whatever you have, and keep your pantry shelf clearer and your crumb jar fuller simultaneously)
>
> chops or grinds nuts
>
> blends things with ice cream for good desserts (see page 127).

Now for some good habits.

In a spirit of idle inquiry once, I asked a couple of friends if there were one thing they wished they'd had the good sense to do when they got married. One said, Marry somebody else. The other said she wished, very much, that she had done what her sister had done.

Early on, it seems, her sister had established a tradition: on one day of the week (she chose Sunday) she didn't cook. It was simply a fact of life in that household. Mother didn't cook on Sundays, any more than the mail came on Sundays. The members of the family simply coped for themselves, using Saturday night's leftovers and whatever else was around. This strengthened their characters, the sister felt, as well as giving her a refreshing oasis to look forward to every weekend.

But my friend ruefully admitted that she's finding it hard to start a tradition after ten years.

There are some other good habits, however, which you can start at any time.

If your grocery load includes tomatoes, you can start water boiling in a saucepan as you put things away. Drop the tomatoes in it, leave them about forty-five seconds, and *then* put them in the refrigerator. The skins will slip off easily when you get around to using the tomatoes, and a skinless tomato always adds a nice touch. That's a good time to process the greenery, too, according to your fashion.

Another good habit, for the preoccupied cook, concerns baking or mixing anything that requires a number of ingredients. If you set them all forth on the kitchen counter and remove the tops, and then *replace* each top the moment you add the ingredient, you're less apt to add something twice or omit it altogether.

Take pantry shelves. They can become so cluttered that finding anything is more trouble than it's worth. This is especially likely if you have high shelves that don't make efficient use of the cubic space. If you can find a two-by-four board that will fit into the cupboard, you can set it on two tall empty baked bean [6] cans, one at each end. That makes an additional shelf for short cans, like tuna and clams. (You can't call this a habit, exactly, but it is a good idea.)

If you ever run out of instant potatoes and need a potato masher, a pop bottle makes a good one. Too, the rim of a cheese glass is good for gently crushing any berries or other fruit you want to be juicy but not soupy. Hold the cheese glass by its bottom, then proceed with delicacy.

And so we come to the matter of new food products.

First off, a thing to beware of, if it costs extra, is the new food product that solves problems you didn't know you had. Advertisers like to invent food problems the way they invent diseases.

For instance, salad dressing that's "homogenized to cling to greens." If you haven't noticed that yours has been sliding off, there is no clear advantage for you here.

Or round spaghetti. If the long kind is a challenge to you, and cheaper, keep on buying it; and if the children have trouble with theirs, chop it up for them.

Indeed, the flood of new food preparations can be con-

[6] Or pineapple juice or tomato juice. That part doesn't matter.

fusing in many ways. You read, for instance, a recipe calling
for, say, marinated peach halves.

Marinated in what? you wonder, crossly. Soy sauce? Maple
syrup? Do they come in a can? You never saw them at *your*
grocer's, and by the time you finish wondering, you don't
care if you never do.

Accomplished home-economics people sometimes assume
that their audience knows more than it does; and for this,
as Socrates said in another context, we may gently blame
them.

Still, we mustn't blame them too much. Many of us lead
sheltered lives where new groceries are concerned. Because
our busy little minds are elsewhere, we tend to trundle
down the same old aisles at the grocer's, buying the same
old products. This can go on for years, and the home
economists, meanwhile, grow tired of explaining that you
can find canned green chilies in most well-stocked grocery
stores, just as you do biscuit mix.

All this is a shame, because so many of the new or newer
products are right down our culinary alley.

For example, bacon that pops out of your toaster crisp
and hot, leaving not a droplet of grease behind it, can be
well worth the extra 10% it costs if you hate to wash skillets
and if you think the bacon tastes good.

Or consider the new freeze-dried things, like the green
bell peppers that come chopped in tidy jars and don't need
refrigerating. Having a green pepper on tap at the right
moment can be a problem, because menus so often change
without notice, owing to circumstances beyond one's control. On Friday night you find—when you get around to using the pepper that was supposed to be the Sunday pepper
last week—that it isn't the pepper it used to be. Freeze-dried
peppers circumvent situations like this and are therefore
an economy.

(Apparently they haven't quite perfected the freeze-dried
fruits-in-cereals, which are still too expensive for how they
taste. So are the complete freeze-dried entrees available now,
mainly at good outdoor stores. A 32-ounce beef stew weighs
only 6 ounces before you prepare it, which makes it handy
for packing upcountry. But unless your food-storage space
at home is limited to one kitchen drawer, upcountry is where
it belongs.)

On the other hand, you occasionally find products that
make you wonder how you ever in the world made out with-

out them. I put the dried grated orange and lemon rind in this category, along with the minced dried onions.

Handy, too, are the packaged preseasoned rice or pasta mixtures: saffron, curry, Parmesan, and so forth. Even though they're no barn-burners, they improve when you reflect upon how easy they were. And if the production was almost good but frail-flavored, you can hit it next time with some more of its basic flavoring and a lump of butter. (If the basic flavoring is curry, simmer the curry *in* the butter for a few minutes before you add it.)

Ditto for the good-flavored shrimp soup containing two shrimps per can: add a can of drained rinsed shrimp. And add a small jar of boned chicken to your chicken à la king.

Only one more example from hundreds: consider the bitter baking chocolate, ready-melted, in aluminum-foil packets. Whatever chocolate-sauce recipe you have been using, you may happily stop it now, and just mix, in a saucepan over low heat

> 1 2-ounce packet of ready-melted chocolate
> with
> ⅓ cup white cane syrup.

When it's hot through, add a touch of sherry, if you like. With or without, it is a first-class chocolate sauce, better than downtown.

But it is fruitless to do more than touch upon the swiftly shifting food picture. I doubt if anyone is wholly up with it, including the biggest frozen, canned, or ready-mixed people. Truly, we live in a food-minded age, as well as a scientific one, and the result is a marvel a minute—some major, some minor, and some even bad-tasting marvels you wouldn't want to keep up with anyway.

Still, there are two things it is wise to do.

One is to make an eagle-eyed exploratory expedition to a good grocery every month or so when one is in a lively, eagle-eyed mood, solely to see what's new.

The other is to allow, consciously, a fair margin in the budget for basic research: buying and trying new products to see if they're worth buying again, as many certainly are.

Also, these experimental monies (one says monies when speaking of funds devoted to serious purposes) can be employed to compare various brands of the same thing to see which is best. Or which, though all right, is wildly extravagant for what it is, unless you want to end up a fiscal mess.

(One says fiscal instead of financial for grave situations like this.)

Then jot it on the blackboard, so you don't get fooled again. There are several pumpkin-pie fillings on the market, for instance, including one in an especially pretty can that makes a remarkably vile pie. For quite a while that's the one I kept buying, till I finally wrote it large on the kitchen wall with a skull and crossbones underneath.

In a word, we can make an effort, when we remember to, while keeping in mind that Science will in all probability stay ahead of us. We will continue to trot along behind, like fat-legged tots on a picnic. But we do see a lot of pretty things along the way.

CHAPTER 5

Dinner, Can't We Take Them Out to?

BUT SOMETIMES YOU CAN'T

"The hostess must be like the duck—calm and unruffled on the surface, and paddling like hell underneath."
—ANONYMOUS

Unfortunately, you entertain to pay people back or to honor them, or both, as well as to get the silver polished once in a while, and you cannot honor people satisfactorily with a pride of hot dogs. Some work is expected of you, and perhaps something a little unusual.

There is nothing precisely exotic in this chapter. When you hate to cook, you don't try to keep up with the Joneses; you only hope you can stay away from the Browns. But you will find here, once we clear away the canapés, five somewhat special dinners. Each one, it is hoped, will fill a particular need.

In fact, these dinners should take care of things for quite some time. You don't entertain that much at home, for one thing. And when you do, your first thought is usually Roast Beef, because it is the easiest and most people like it. If only it weren't so expensive, and didn't require accurate timing, and were as easy to serve and eat as a casserole, and no one observed any meatless days, you would probably serve it all the time.

But it is, and it does, and it isn't, and they do; so you don't.

Before we go into these five dinners, let's consider the canapé.

It is easy to overlook the canapé, and often advisable. They are bothersome to make. And they have disadvantages for the guest, who stands there growing fuller and often spottier, depending on the consistency of the dip (see a little farther along).

There is a difference between the sexes where canapés are concerned. Women like them pretty, and men usually just don't like them. C. S. Lewis once remarked that the middle-aged male has great powers of passive resistance. But I've noticed that males of all ages are talented at not reaching for the marinated fiddleheads[1] and other nonappetizers. It was a man, I am sure, who invented the bowl of dry-roasted nuts, and a woman who invented Dilled Bean Roll-ups.

The following three canapés[2] and three dips are included from a sense of duty, and because they're good to know about when it's cocktails only, not dinner.

THE HOT DILLED BEAN ROLL-UP

(This is cheap and exceptionally good. Libby dills the beans —some smaller packers do, too—and they're in cans at the supermarket. If you don't find them in Canned Vegetables, look in Hors d'Oeuvres.)

[1] Known also as cinnamon fern. You find them growing along shady streams or canned in big groceries.

[2] Plus one more that I'm diffident about putting anywhere but in a footnote: You mix smooth peanut butter with catsup until each loses its identity—about half and half, but keep tasting. The resultant new flavor is good and hard to analyze. Spread it on crackers or Melba toast.

Trim the crusts from thin slices of white bread and flatten the bread with a rolling pin.

Then spread them with mayonnaise and roll up a dilled bean in each. Refrigerate them for an hour—longer wouldn't hurt—then cut them in half, or in thirds, according to how many you want. Brush them with melted butter and broil about 4 inches from a hot broiler, turning them once.

You can even broil them in the morning, if you like, and reheat them just before you need them, for about ten minutes at 325°.

THE HANDIEST HOT CANAPÉ

(*Good to know about because the ingredients are nearly always on hand, and it tastes far better than it sounds.*)

Put a few onion rings, or thinly sliced green onions, on rounds of Melba toast or any good cracker.

Put a dab of mayonnaise (not salad dressing) on each, and slip them under the broiler till the mayonnaise sizzles.

THE SECOND-HANDIEST CANAPÉ

(*One doesn't always have white tuna around, but it's easy to get. This dull-sounding recipe is another proof of a point mentioned earlier, that you can't ever tell.*)

1 can white tuna	coarse-ground pepper
4 to 6 chopped green onions	mayonnaise

Put the tuna in a bowl, then add the onions and mayonnaise a little at a time till it's the right consistency. Add more ground pepper than you think you should, tasting as you go.

You can broil this on toast rounds or crackers. Or add more mayonnaise and use it as a dip.

The dip

The important thing about The Dip is its consistency. When it is stiff enough to break the chips, it lasts longer, because soon the bowl of solid shards discourages people. Still, the too-liquid type can discourage people, too. You want a sure eye here, and a light touch.

RADISH AND BUTTER SEMIDIP

Mash Roquefort or blue cheese with an equal amount of butter. Cream it thoroughly and put it in a bowl.

Put the bowl on a plate and surround it with scrubbed radishes, their green handles left on, and some good crackers (for people who like radishes but radishes don't like them, as they are usually happy to explain.) You must also put a knife on the plate, so that the other people can apply a dab of cheese to the radish, which works better than dunking.

SHRIMP CREAM DIP
(Delicate and rather pretty)

Combine these things:

3-ounce package cream cheese, mashed

can of frozen shrimp soup, thawed but undiluted

1 teaspoon Worcestershire

chopped ripe olives, as many as you like

½ teaspoon curry powder.

If it needs any thinning, whole milk is all right. Raw cauliflowerets are good to dip with. So are chips.

MYSTERY BEAN DIP

(The mystery is why you'd bother with it, because—though it's quite good—the other two don't take any cooking. The only possible answer is that whoever gave you your chafing dish is coming for cocktails.)

First, grate a good-sized onion on the middle-sized grater. Then sauté it in 2 tablespoons of butter. Now add and mix:

1 can condensed black bean soup, undiluted

½ teaspoon garlic powder

½ pound grated Cheddar

2 tablespoons sherry

a good spatter of Tabasco.

You can keep it, over gently boiling water, in the top part of a double boiler. Then get out the chafing dish.

There is one other canapé situation we should touch on here. Occasionally, as in the jolly family get-together we're presently coming to, children are around during the cocktail hour.

This brings up the matter of Mother's Lead Balloons, which is the generic term for anything good and faintly unusual when offered to children, who will regard it with wary little jungle eyes.

There is no reason children should eat canapés anyway, unless it is a long cocktail hour or unless you suspect that the little reactionaries won't like the dinner any better (containing, as it does, something as exotic as anchovies).

A good thing to prepare, in this case, is

PATRICIAN PIGLETS

makes 16

a tube of refrigerated crescent rolls
a package of 1-inch cocktail hot dogs (you could use
   Vienna Sausage but the children won't like it. Or
   regular hot dogs, chunked, but they wouldn't look
   so—well—cute).

Unwrap the dough triangles, cut each in half the long way,
spread lightly with prepared hot-dog mustard, and roll up a
piglet in each. You won't need toothpicks. Bake for ten minutes at 375°.

You can give these to the children along with a good
punch. Then you might not have to feed them dinner at all.

And now to the five dinners.

1. THE STRETCHABLE JUST-A-FORK DINNER

(*It is remarkable how a one-tool plateful seems to simplify
serving and eating, whether it actually does or not.*)

Manny's Lamb Stew
Ready Caesar Salad (page 98)   Prebuttered Hot Rolls
any Dessert you bought or any dessert
you made yesterday, such as
Immediate Fudge Cake (page 128)
Wine   Coffee

It is with a certain embarrassed doggedness that I feature
here Manny's Lamb Stew, from another book of mine, *The
I Hate to Housekeep Book*.[8] I do it because I've yet to find
another recipe with so many pluses for unwilling cooks.

It is simple, easily doubled, tripled, or quadrupled, in addition to being cheap, preparable in advance, and depend-
ably good, with a faint French accent. Like a good sheath,
you can dress it up or down, depending on what you put
with it, and it seems to fit the kitchen or the candlelit dining
room equally well.

[8] Harcourt, Brace & World, Inc., 1962. Fawcett Crest paperback
edition, 1965.

MANNY'S LAMB STEW

6-8 servings

2½ pounds of lean stewing lamb—shoulder is good—
cut in edible-size pieces. Have the butcher bone it
for you and ask him please to trim off the fat.

Brown this in 4 tablespoons of olive oil, using a heavy
skillet with a lid.

Then take the lamb out and pour out most of the oil,
leaving just enough for sautéing

        1 peeled, coarsely chopped onion
        1 crushed garlic clove.

Do that, then put the lamb back in, along with

2 tablespoons flour	1½ teaspoons salt
1½ cups chicken consommé	¼ teaspoon pepper
(canned, instant, powdered,	¼ teaspoon marjoram
or 2 cubes in 1½ cups	1 crumbled bay leaf
water)	2 tablespoons lemon juice.

Simmer this for five minutes with the skillet lid on. Add

    4 carrots, scraped and cut in chunks[4]
    4 medium potatoes, peeled and quartered
    1 1-pound can small white onions, drained and rinsed.

Simmer it all, covered, for twenty-five minutes. STOP HERE.
Reheat it, and, just before serving, sprinkle chopped parsley
on top.

This entire Dinner #1, by the way, is a good one to bring
guests home to. A friend of mine went to a hanging, at the
local art museum, then brought the artist and her friends
back with her. Before she left home, she had set small tables,
with a bottle of wine on each. When she returned, she heated
the stew, put the previously buttered rolls in the oven, found
the salad dressing and salad greens, and dinner was ready in
one drink.

The salad could, of course, be any green salad, though its
dressing should contain lemon juice instead of vinegar, as a
small elegant echo of the stew. It's those elegant echoes that
add up.

---

[4] Chunked carrots are considered smarter than sliced carrots.

2. THE JOLLY FAMILY GET-TOGETHER

(Of All My Husband's Relatives, I Like Myself the Best)

This one—also known as the Out-of-Season Unstuffed Turkey Dinner—has numerous advantages. Turkey tastes much better, for one thing, away from the holiday season. Moreover, an unstuffed turkey couldn't be much easier to cook, and it feeds large numbers.

The important thing is to get away from the Thanksgiving taste, which will then seem fresher when November rolls around. Consider this bird only as pounds of light and dark turkey meat, which you might have bought at the delicatessen for vastly more money.

> A frozen Turkey, thawed and roasted unstuffed[5]
> Mushroom Business (page 80)
> Good Spinach Salad (page 99)
> Hot Fruit Compote served cold (page 130)
> Pot-de-Chocolat (page 122)

One caution: There is nothing spontaneous about a frozen turkey dinner, and the bigger the bird, the less spontaneity you've got to work with. This table of thawing might prevent trouble.

To thaw a frozen turkey on the refrigerator shelf:

> 4 to 12 pounds—1 to 2 days
> 12 to 20 pounds—2 to 3 days
> 20 to 24 pounds—3 to 4 days

You cut the time in half, nearly, by putting it in a pan (it's apt to drip) and leaving it at room temperature. The closed unheated oven is a good place. But be sure to leave enough time so it's thoroughly thawed.

The process is this:

First, decide when you want to serve dinner. Then find a scratch pad and figure out how long you'll have to cook the turkey. The experts say:

> 20 minutes per pound at 325° for 16 pounds or less
> 15 minutes per pound at 325° for a larger bird.

Then add twenty minutes out of the oven for the turkey's juices to settle before it's carved, and a very handy twenty minutes that can be.

---

[5] Of course it needn't be frozen. But fresh or frozen, the cooking rule is the same.

So, at the proper distance from dinner, take the innards out of whatever cavity they're in—at either end or both.

Now tie the legs together neatly, and tie a string around the whole bird to keep the wings close to the chest. (You don't need to sew anything up or skewer anything together.)

Brush the bird generously with melted vegetable shortening. Put it in a roasting pan and cover it with aluminum foil— just bend a piece of it over the turkey, tucking it loosely around.

Cook it till thirty minutes short of the time you figured. Then remove the foil permanently, so he'll brown a bit.

This is a good time to test it. Gently pull its leg to see if it's getting loose in the socket. Remember that turkeys are like people, and they can't all be counted on to follow the rules. If the leg comes off in your hand—which is only the remotest of possibilities—the turkey has had it, so get it out of there. It's overdone, though edible.

But chances are excellent that the time you figured will be right, if you didn't flunk third-grade arithmetic. So let it roast the remaining thirty minutes. Then let it sit the twenty minutes you allowed for sitting time, outside the oven.

Carve it and serve it. There.

About desserts here: a box of good chocolates would be as good as the Pot-de-Chocolat, come to think of it, and easier. You must remember that no matter how simple the menu is, entertaining is still like alligator-rassling, involving everything you've got, and you must simplify where you can.

Something not to worry about, by the way, is lipstick. It is appalling, though not serious, how much glamour comes off on the napkin. But you merely pick up the napkins gingerly by one corner and put them aside till washday. Then, about fifteen minutes before washing a load, rub salad oil on each red stain till it soaks through the material, and put them in the wash. The oil melts the lipstick, you see, and the laundering removes the oil.

3. FAT MAN'S SHRIMP DINNER

(Rich and good, easy to double, and handy for Friday night. You needn't have another cooked vegetable, because of the spinach with the shrimp.)

Fat Man's Shrimp
any Salad involving tomatoes and onions
hot ready-mix Corn Bread or hot
Crescent Rolls or frozen
heated Croissants
something you bought for Dessert
or Brown Sugar Apple Pie (page 121)

FAT MAN'S SHRIMP

6 *servings*

Cook 2 packages of frozen chopped spinach according to directions, and let it drain in a colander while you mix 1 cup of sour cream with 2 cans of undiluted condensed cream of mushroom soup.

Add to it

> 8-ounce can browned-in-butter mushrooms, drained
> (or ½ pound fresh ones, sautéed in butter)
> ½ cup grated Parmesan
> ½ teaspoon dry mustard.

Heat it through, then add

> 2 cups cooked shrimp (fresh, canned, or frozen).

Now put a layer of the spinach in a casserole dish, then a layer of the shrimp mixture, and so on, hopefully ending with the shrimp. Sprinkle some grated coconut on top for a gala note. STOP HERE. It will toast as you bake the dish later, uncovered, at 350° for half an hour.

If you're out of coconut, you can use very coarse buttered crumbs, though it isn't so gala.

4. THE VERY CASUAL LOAF DINNER

This is for seemingly random invitations. For instance, if a couple has been chauffeuring your child to Little League practice, you might invite them to stop in for supper next time they bring him home.

In truth, you can't be quite so easygoing as you sound, because you must get the French bread and spread it with numerous things. But it can be done early on.

This is a welcome change from the usual hamburger-pizza loaf, and it's good with beer, or a cup of soup, or a jug of lemonade, with fruit for dessert.

LARAMIE LOAF

4-5 servings

Before you split a long loaf of French bread, score it a quarter-inch deep both bottom and top where you intend to slice it later. *Then* split it.

On side #1 spread butter.

On side #2, spread a mixture of

    2½ cups grated yellow cheese
    1 3-ounce package of cream cheese
    ¼ cup mayonnaise
    2 teaspoons prepared mustard
    1½ teaspoons Worcestershire sauce
    some ripe olives, chopped

You're not done yet. On that, sprinkle

    4 chopped green onions, with a lot of the green
    2 thinly sliced tomatoes
    10 slices crisp bacon.

Put the top on (side #1), wrap it loosely in aluminum foil, twisting the ends but leaving the top open so it won't steam. STOP HERE. Bake it in a 350° oven for fifteen minutes.

Cut it according to the earlier scoring and serve it.

5. THE INTERESTING CHICKEN DINNER

4 servings

For any restive Roast Beef Regulars, this could provide a change of pace. The marrons are expensive but the chicken is cheap.

Chestnut Chicken
Saffron Rice (comes prepared)
or Mother Bradford's Rice (page 153)
Asparagus with Crumb Topping (page 106)
simplest possible Green Salad
Pot-de Strawberry (page 123)

CHESTNUT CHICKEN

Flour enough chicken breasts for four people. Brown them all over in a skillet, in about ¼ cup of oil. Put them in a good-sized casserole, and make a sauce:

Stir 2 tablespoons of cornstarch into ¼ cup of flour till it's smooth. Then add 2 cups of cold water, ¼ teaspoon of tarragon, 1 teaspoon of Ac'cent (MSG), and ½ teaspoon of salt. Over low heat stir it constantly, I'm afraid, till it's about as thick as medium cream sauce. Or put it in a double boiler so you don't have to be so careful. Then add

> 1 tablespoon lime juice
> 1 teaspoon grated lime rind
> 1 cup drained coarsely chopped *marrons glacés* don't wash them, just drain them, because you want a touch of the syrup)
> 1 cup sour cream.

Stir it all together, pour it over the chicken, cover it, STOP HERE, and bake it for an hour at 350°.

Finally, one more item belongs in this chapter, a kind of a mushroom business. I was given the recipe; my friend said it was to serve with any roasted meat instead of pan-roasted potatoes, and, she continued, you can prepare it the day before. When I asked why one *should* serve anything but good easy pan-roasted potatoes, she looked at me oddly and dropped the subject. Uneasily, I sensed that she knew something I didn't.

When I eventually tall-talked myself into trying it, I found it was extraordinarily handsome. Also it was remarkably good, and it took only twenty-five minutes to make instead of the hour I'd expected.

Serving it as I did, at an eat-where-you-land buffet, I found, too, that it's simpler for guests—no smashing, buttering, salting, and peppering, which is the accepted attack on an oven-roasted potato in my part of the corn patch.

All in all, the experience was as unsettling as having your horoscope prediction come true. Still, I'm glad it happened.

MUSHROOM BUSINESS

6-8 *servings*

Sauté ½ to 1 pound of fresh mushrooms, coarsely sliced, in butter, just enough so they start to smell like mushrooms. (Don't peel them or wash them in water before you do this; just wipe them with a damp rag.)

Butter three slices of white bread, cut them in 1-inch squares, and put them in a casserole dish.

Combine the mushrooms with

½ cup each of
    chopped onion

mayonnaise
¾ teaspoon salt

chopped celery   ¼ teaspoon pepper
chopped green pepper

and put it on the bread squares.

Now cut three more slices of buttered bread the same way.
Put them in next, and over it pour 2 eggs slightly beaten with
1½ cups milk.

It doesn't matter when you do this—the morning before, if
you like—just so it's refrigerated at least one hour.

Finally, an hour before you want to serve it, spoon a can
of undiluted mushroom soup over it, and two more slices of
bread, diced smaller. Bake it at 300° for sixty to seventy
minutes, or 325° for fifty to sixty minutes. About ten minutes
before it's done, sprinkle some grated yellow cheese on top.

Crisis, coping in a

Some of the best fiction of our time is written by well-
meaning domestic-science experts about how to cope in domestic emergencies. For example, if you bring guests back
after the Big Game and find the oven cold and your turkey
uncooked. Or similar crises that demand more than merely
substituting a tablespoon of vinegar.

Contrary to what you may have read about it, it has
been my experience that these seemingly hopeless situations
actually are. And when you, as hostess, do something gallant
and inventive, the guests will probably wish you hadn't.

They were primed for turkey, you see. All the way from
the stadium to your house they could fairly smell it, brown,
succulent, bursting with its juices. And even if their taste buds
are pickled at that point, as they well may be, they are not
going to like that brave lima-bean–peanut-butter casserole
you created out of what was around. Though it's reasonably
good, it will suffer by comparison with what they might have
been eating.

In these major crises, then—which are fortunately as few
and far between as the nuts in a Bingo-prize fruitcake—one
might as well be more gallant still and take the group out
to dinner.

I believe the automatic oven timer is one reason the
Diners' Club was invented.

> *"Omnia potest perdere,*
>   *or, freely translated,*
> *You can lose 'em all."*
>   —J. P. MULLER

CHAPTER 6

Fat, Some of My Best Friends Are

AND WHAT THE OTHER ONES DO

*"The huge Brontosaurus of the Jurassic Period
stayed in shallow water to take the weight off his feet."*
—BRYAN PATTERSON

Cooking—if you ever noticed—involves you with food to
rather an alarming extent: shopping for it, driving it about,
carrying it in, washing it, wiping it, putting it away, hunting
for it. . . .

Especially when you're dieting, you should have as little to
do with all this as possible, for it only makes the dieting
harder. The delicious-sounding recipes and earnest menus in
low-calorie cookbooks make sense only if you have a cook
who cooks them for you. Otherwise, as in the case of the

driver who cracked his car up while fastening his seat belt, overconscientiousness can do you in.

I once spent an 800-calorie-per-day week at a so-called beauty farm, from which one emerges hungry if not beautiful. The food, what there was of it, was certainly good, and the cook was certainly fat.

Not that the food was marvelous beyond belief. I'll never forget the night the baked onion stuffed with cheese turned into a revolting baked turnip stuffed with God-knows-what, in my very mouth. Often, as I munched the papaya cubes and celery root that passed for canapés, I pondered the immortal words of Maxim's Louis Vaudable: "Dieticians are the worst enemy of the great cuisine; it is impossible to have low calories in excellent food."

Clearly, then, if a dieter cooks much of anything, in this ready-packaged diet-food day, she has pixies at the bottom of her pea patch.

Or a family to feed.

Then there's another situation that can develop: perhaps it is her husband who goes on a diet. Not that the reluctant cook gives up early here. At first, she stocks the refrigerator with fruit and cans of liquid diet for her husband. As the days go by, she watches him uneasily, taking his pulse now and then.

But if he's shooting at a ten- or fifteen-pound target, she may eventually heave a sigh that blows the Sunday papers out the window, then go dig out the Teflon frying pan.

Nor is her reaction wholly unselfish, especially if she's noticed lately that she's been asking a good deal of her stretch pants. She may get wholeheartedly into the act then, and feed him fascinating tidbits along with the yogurt, like the fact that you lose weight when you eat a hard-boiled egg[1] but take

---

[1] For the reason that your body has to work so hard to digest the hard-boiled egg that it actually uses up more calories than the egg contributes (whereas a soft-boiled egg digests easily and leaves you with a plus). According to Dr. Heinz Humplik, a Viennese specialist in these matters, a hard-boiled egg represents 80 calories. Yet it requires 92 calories to digest it. Therefore, you've lost weight just in the process of eating it. If you eat 4 hard-boiled eggs, you will lose 48 calories just because you ate them. (And just think, if you'd eat 100 hard-boiled eggs every day, you'd be minus 1200 calories each day and presently fade away to nothing! Perhaps it doesn't pay to examine these things too thoroughly.)

However, the same thing holds true of a whole orange compared with a glass of orange juice. And liquor—in spite of the Drinking

on some plus calories with a soft-boiled one, not even counting the piece of toast you generally eat with it.

This chapter will contain a few recipes for easy low-calorie goodies, or Not-So-Goodies, which I consider a better name. Mainly, though, it will contain more important things, like how to make your own fatrecal in the privacy of your own house (in case you run out), and how to start a stretch of dieting, and the fastest way to get your waistline back, and a rule of thumb for finding how much you can eat to stay the size you'd like to be, and a rule of belly button, for determining whether you're absolutely enormous, in case you haven't looked in the looking glass lately.

Or at least I think it will contain all these things. Sometimes it's hard to see around the bend. Or over the belly button.

Now, more women diet needlessly than men, who usually wait for word from a doctor or until something won't fasten. But sometimes a big-boned woman will expect herself to weigh the same as a small-boned woman the same height.

However, bone size has a good deal to do with it. The rule for everyone is 100 pounds for the first five feet in height. Then medium-framed people are allowed five pounds each for the additional inches, while small-framed people get fewer and big-framed people get more. (The best clue to the size of the frame is the size of the hands and the feet.)

More often though, people diet unnecessarily because everything from television to fashion ads has made it seem wicked to cast a shadow. This wild emaciated look appeals to some women, though not to many men, who are seldom seen pinning up a *Vogue* illustration in a machine shop.

Also, the reducing-parlor people and the beauty spas keep screaming things like "Ten pounds thinner is ten years younger!" the same way the cosmetics people insist that the fountain of youth is a bucket of wrinkle cream.[2]

Man's Diet furore—is a cinch to digest. Alcohol converts more easily to fat, say the experts, than most things. So it seems, at this writing, that though all calories are equal, some are more equal than others.

[2] But, as you may have noticed, a fat old lady looks younger than a skinny old lady; and all recent photographs of cosmetics-company founders prove that after a certain point, one has a choice between dry wrinkles or oily wrinkles, which isn't much of a choice, but there it is.

It's easy to figure out how many calories you can eat and maintain your proper weight (though you'd have to eat fewer than that, of course, to get down to it.) You multiply your proper weight by 15 calories. If you want to stay 116, that's 15 x 116, or 1740 you have as a daily allowance.

To learn if you're truly obese, pinch yourself just below the belly button. If the distance between your fingers is over 1½ inches for a woman or 1 inch for a man, you sure are. This is up to you and the doctor then, if you want to try to do something about it, though some people don't.

I know an intelligent fat man who says he's well aware that fat people generally don't live as long as thin ones. Still, he says, he sees no point in living thirty miserable years— this man enjoys his food and gains quickly—in order to live another ten miserable years. And he says that from what he's seen of the far end of the sunset trail, he doesn't think too much of it anyway.

Too, some fat people may not be so overweight as they think they are. Some encouraging research is underway on this, as reported by Dr. Carl C. Seltzer, research associate in physical anthropology at Harvard University's School of Public Health.

The way to find out how much you can weigh without affecting the length of your lifetime involves taking the cube root of your weight and dividing it into your height in inches. This plunge into higher mathematics defeats my application of the Old Math, though it results in a considerably higher possible weight than the ordinary actuarial tables give you.

For instance, for a woman 5 foot 3, with a large frame, the actuarial table lists 142. But Dr. Seltzer's says she can weigh 157. A large-framed man over twenty-five, 5 foot 10, should not allow himself to weigh more than 179, say the actuarial tables. But Dr. Seltzer gives him 216.

For anyone who knows how to figure cube root, this might be an interesting path to stroll.

The approaching diet suggestions assume that no one is going to change food habits very much, for hardly anyone ever does. Even jockeys and mannequins, who must weigh in skinny in order to work, usually eat themselves bowlegged, once they get off the reservation.

What we'll consider here is what some wag has termed the Rhythm Method of Girth Control. It involves the 5- to

15-pound overage[3] that you keep dropping and picking up again like a familiar suitcase. The Rhythm Method has the clear merit of letting people feel virtuous while they are being Spartan, and sinful while they are living it up, both very pleasant feelings.

Some RM people are more organized about it than others. I know a couple who lives a mainly watercress-and-skim-milk life every January and February, then shifts to whipped cream and lobster for the rest of the year. And I know a woman who doesn't eat on Mondays, just the other days. And I know a man who diets every afternoon between lunch and dinnertime.

The rest diet somewhat spasmodically, often in the late spring when the buds and the buttons start to pop. They don't see their doctors, either; they just see the new bathing suits. And they usually depend, for openers, on the Fad Diet.

Though greatly maligned, the Fad Diet has its virtues. There is one for everybody, regardless of race, creed, or color, and it's something to get up in the morning for, just to see what today's is going to be: booze it up, eat it up, live high on the fat, low on the sugar, or heavy on the egg noodles.

Every Fad Diet roars in like a lion and sneaks out like a lamb chop with a slice of pineapple, which was the start of the whole thing, some decades ago. And at each and every Fad Diet the A.M.A. wags its whiskers and says, "No, you've simply got to stop eating so much."

But I can't believe Fad Diets are all bad. No one in his right mind could stay on one for longer than three days,[4] and if you're healthy you can stand anything for three days, even no food at all.

Moreover, fad dieting for three days gives you a great psychological start. When your digestive system is insulted like this, it quickly gets the message that things are rough and apt to get no better for a while. Then it settles down to the longer low-calorie pull.

The most interesting Fad Diet I've heard about lately, by the way, is the Wolf-all-you-like-of-whatever-you-like-for-two-minutes-three-times-a-day Diet. Depending on what you chose

---

[3] About the distance between manufacturers' clothes sizes.

[4] Though I did know one girl in her wrong mind who lived on pears and cottage cheese for ten months and lost 40 pounds that included her gall bladder. She gained the 40 pounds back but not the gall bladder.

to wolf, I think you could also charge admission at feeding time.

The big thing is to choose your Fad Diet carefully, as you do your television repairman, and get the one that's right for *you.* Generally speaking, it should emphasize the foods you like best.

For instance, the ice-cream-and-poundcake routine below is good for the person who likes sweets, for he'll be a little sick of them by the end of the second day.

Each of these diets will lose 3 to 5 pounds for you in three days, a little less in two.

1. *All the vanilla ice cream and poundcake you want.* (But no sauce, no nuts, no nonsense.)
2. *Steak, prunes, and coffee.*
   Breakfast: 5 stewed prunes, 1 cup of coffee
   Lunch: a big steak, fat and all, 1 cup of coffee
   Dinner: same as lunch.
3. *Nothing but fruit juice—any kind—and tea.*
4. *Milk and bananas.*
   For each meal, 1 glass of whole milk, 2 bananas.
5. *Pear, cottage cheese, and lettuce salad,* with 1 tablespoon of French dressing, three times a day.
6. *Only liquids till dinner* (nonalcoholic, and not more than a cup of milk, with artificial sweeteners in drinks).
   For dinner: lean meat, 2 vegetables (not potato), fresh or diet-pack fruit.
7. *The mainly protein pattern.*
   Breakfast: 3 hard-boiled eggs, coffee
   Lunch: ½ cupful each of raisins and shelled nuts
   Dinner: lean meat, 2 vegetables (not potato), and coffee.
8. *900-calorie liquid diet* (4 commercial cans a day).
9. *Painless Plasma,* to make yourself.
   Mix together, every morning:
   1½ cups skim-milk powder
   1 quart water
   3 tablespoons honey
   2 tablespoons corn oil
   Whatever flavoring you like—instant coffee, brandy, vanilla, nutmeg.
   Drink it all in one day, spacing it as you prefer.
10. *Health Juice,* to make yourself.
    Mix, chill, and drink as above:

> 1 cup pineapple juice
> 1 can (10½-ounce) evaporated milk
> 6 tablespoons dextrose
> 2 tablespoons corn oil
> ½ cup brewer's yeast.

After this three- or two-day start comes a few hours of nearly unbearable virtue. All orange juice looks evil because it's 50 calories more than the same amount of tomato juice. You regard from a tall skinny summit the people who eat the buns surrounding their hamburgers (at a good 150 calories per bun) and who order a Whisky Sour (at 225) instead of an ounce of bourbon (at 100).

You must get over this promptly, for pride now is the devil's own pitfall. Before you know it you'll be right back in the soup, a good calorie-loaded cream of shrimp, for instance, at 260 per cupful.

So you decide quickly on the system you're going to follow for the next few weeks. This, too, is an individual matter, though mainly you think back to what you did last spring and do it again.

Easiest of all is to cut out a few lardy habits that total around 500 calories a day. For instance, just omitting

a Danish pastry	150
cream and sugar in 3 cups of coffee	100
one 2½-ounce dry Martini[5]	180
one slice of buttered toast	100

would lose a pound a week for the person who does it.

More impatient types, who want to lose two pounds a week, also omit all desserts, breads, potatoes, or whatever formerly made a meal satisfying. Or they cleave to the liquid diet for breakfast and lunch, then have a 600-calorie dinner of lean meat and vegetables.

One of the neatest diets I've heard about was recently given to a friend of mine by his doctor, who wanted him to shake 15. "No fat, no wheat," said the doctor briskly. Which my friend obediently omitted, and he lost the 15 pounds in five weeks.

It is wise, by the way, to stop at the newsstand and buy another calorie-counting booklet to replace the one that probably got lost after last spring's go-around.

---

[5] If you prefer to hang onto the Martini and will take a brisk half-hour's walk, the walk will burn up 150 calories and you'll come out about the same, though merrier.

This can prevent mistakes, like baking-powder biscuits, only one of which—with enough butter to make it worth the powder that blew it up—costs about 75 calories. That's expensive, unless you're truly devoted to baking-powder biscuits. For the same calorie price, you could buy an ounce of brandy, or 15 Nabisco sugar wafers, or 20 asparagus spears with a little butter and lemon, any one of which might do more for your psyche. And only 5 fried grasshoppers cost 225 calories. So that's something else to beware of.

Another booklet almost essential for getting somewhere quickly, like back into your clothes, is *How to Exercise without Moving a Muscle*[6] by Victor Obeck, Professor of Physical Education and Director of Athletics at New York University.

These are isometric exercises. They lose you no pounds, only inches. But because clothes sizes are geared to waist rather than weight, Mr. Obeck's six-second waist exercise alone is worth the price of the book.

(In modified form, it is holding your stomach in hard, trying to press it through your backbone, for a slow count of six. Done 10 times a day, it pares you over an inch a month. Until there's nothing extra to pare, of course.)

These exercises are especially nice because they can be done in the car as you drive, at the phone, at the desk, almost anywhere, including bed.

One other good investment, for women, is a good-looking shoe-toter—one of those odd-shaped bags that carries your dress shoes while you walk in comfortable walking shoes to a meeting or a cocktail party. A good plan is to drive to within a mile or two of the place, then switch shoes and walk it from there, with a clear gain of 75 calories burned up for each brisk fifteen minutes.

Now for some words to post on the refrigerator door:
". . . Dr. W. J. Bryan (*founder of the American Institute of Hypnosis*) *concludes that obesity in the U.S. is a result of good food, cooked too well, and eaten in too pleasant an atmosphere. He suggests that auto-suggestion begin at home with worse food, bad atmosphere, and 'maybe a little willful carelessness thrown in which can do as much as medicine in weight control.'* "[7]

[6] Pocket Books, Inc.
[7] *Insider's Newsletter*, October 11, 1965.

And so to the scatter of recipes predicted earlier.

No entrees are given here, for the reason that plain meat, fowl, and fish, baked or broiled or pan fried in a Teflon pan with no fat, are the easiest as well as the lowest in calories. There is little point in doing anything else to them, for the unwilling cook who is dieting—or cooking for someone who is—has problems enough. What we will touch on, ever so lightly, is some appetizers, some hot vegetables, and a few desserts.

1. *How to spoil the appetite before dinner*

You can eat large amounts of these vegetables (previously crisped in ice water):

celery sticks	turnip sticks
carrot strips	radishes
cucumber strips	zucchini strips

They all taste livelier if you sprinkle them with Beau Monde (or a similar) seasoning salt.

Or with them you can serve a

6-CALORIE PER TABLESPOON CLAM DIP

> 1 7-ounce can drained minced clams
> ½ cup diet-type cottage cheese
> dash of Tabasco
> 1 teaspoon instant minced onion
> Worcestershire sauce to taste
> pepper—no salt

Chop the clams even further. Then mix everything up and serve it cold with the vegetables.

Or maybe it would help to eat a

50-CALORIE DEVILED HALF-EGG

Mix the yolk with prepared mustard and a little skim milk. Stuff it back into the egg halves and put the merest squiggle of an anchovy or a sardine on the top.

Or you could serve a

30-CALORIE PER SERVING WINE CONSOMMÉ

6 servings

> 3 cups chicken bouillon

2 tablespoons unflavored gelatin
1 cup dry white wine

Use a little of the cold bouillon to soften the gelatin. Then dissolve it over hot water and add the rest of the bouillon and the wine. Chill it till it's firm, then chop it up, more or less, with a fork, spoon it into bowls, and garnish it with something green—parsley, watercress—plus a lemon slice.

Or you could have as a first course

YOGURT SALAD

Be sure it's the skim-milk yogurt. Mix it sparingly with sliced cucumbers, chopped fresh mint if you have it (but dried will do), lemon juice, and a suspicion of salt.

Or you could simply eat half a head of lettuce before dinner. It tires the jaws and fills the stomach and annoys other people and is a pretty good way to derail a meal.

2. *Some hot vegetables*

With a lean plain entree, these can help dispel the under-privileged feeling. (When the calorie count is mentioned, it means per serving.)

HOT DILL BEANS

Use canned heated string beans, or frozen or fresh cooked till barely tender. Then season, while they steam, with a good teaspoon of chopped dill, preferably fresh, plus 2 tablespoons each of corn oil and dry sherry. Serve quickly.

60-CALORIE BAKED HALF-SPUD

4 *servings*

Bake 2 big potatoes. Cut them in half, scoop out and mash the innards, then mix with

3 tablespoons skim milk
¼ cup diet cottage cheese
1 teaspoon salt
pepper
2 tablespoons green onions
or chives

Pile this back into the potato shells and heat for ten minutes at around 400°.

50-CALORIE EGGPLANT

4 servings

Grease a baking dish with olive oil. In it layer these vegetables till you run out:

> 1 eggplant, sliced thin
> 2 onions, sliced thin
> 2 chopped tomatoes.

Sprinkle it all with a little salt, pepper, and a good pinch of oregano. Bake for forty-five minutes at 350°.

60-CALORIE CHEESE BROCCOLI

4 servings

Cook a package of frozen broccoli according to directions. Then, in saucepan, mix

> ⅓ cup buttermilk
> ⅓ cup Romano cheese

and simmer it over low heat for five minutes, and pour it over the broccoli.

3. *The dessert situation*

Rich desserts, if you like them, are a problem best solved by leaving occasional calorie room for a decent one. The low-calorie gelatin soufflés and so forth are seldom good enough to be worth the work, and the artificially sweetened ones so often taste bitter.

But you can choose what you like from the calorie booklet and allow for it—say, a scoop of vanilla ice cream[8] with a tablespoon of chocolate sauce for 250.

Otherwise, whole fresh fruit or a small can of the dietetic variety does fine. By the way, a sauce that's good on most fruits and berries is

22-CALORIE BANANA WHIP
(*several generous tablespoons per serving*)

Beat an egg white till it's stiff. Then add

> ½ cup ripe mashed bananas
> 1 tablespoon sugar
> slight dash of salt

[8] Unhappily, what is called "Iced Milk" or "Milk Ice," et cetera is nearly as calorie-rich as ice cream. It has less fat but more sugar. So you might as well have ice cream.

and beat some more. Serve it chilled, over fresh peaches, strawberries, raspberries. . . .

And finally to a few Small Comforts:

Dry wine before dinner—about 3½ ounces—contains only 70 calories. That's 110 less than a 2½-ounce dry Martini.

You can be generous with dry wines in your cooking, because it's the alcohol that contains the calories, and it cooks away.

More lemon juice and less butter makes most hot vegetables better anyway.

You can make most sour-cream recipes you like—if you like any—with skim-milk yogurt (115 calories per cupful) instead of sour cream (400 per cupful).

In cooked foods you can't detect the taste of dried skim milk, and it's far more thinning than the whole.

When something needs sweetening, a little vanilla often does it, with no cost in calories.

If you don't like the fake whipped cream that comes in aerosol cans (though some of them are all right), you can extend true whipped cream with beaten egg white, thus lowering the calories, too.

And—as mentioned earlier—Teflon cookware makes cooking fat unnecessary unless you specifically want the taste of the fat.

All these things are good to adopt as habits, of course, if they seem relatively painless, for they can lengthen the span between diet times—from lilac-time to daffodil-time, perhaps, and maybe right on up to roses.

Not that you would want to dispense with the random diet altogether. There is always that good victorious feeling when you lick the situation again, which you certainly wouldn't want to be without.

CHAPTER 7

Greenery,
What to Do with the

WHAT SHOULD YOU TELL YOUR CHILDREN ABOUT MOLDED SALADS?

"The universe is not only queerer than we suppose but queerer than we can suppose."
—J. B. S. HALDANE

According to current thinking, when they're old enough to ask intelligent questions, they're old enough to get straight answers. So you'll simply have to explain to them that in spite of the vast numbers of molded salads made daily, not so many people enjoy them as the children might think (because of the children's own fondness for banana slices in bright pink gelatin).

You may tell them, too, that they're welcome to check this out at any buffet or Town Hall supper. The green salad goes, and the bean salad goes. So does the potato salad and the fruit salad and even that sloppy-looking bowl of coleslaw. But there sits the molded salad, quivering, like the chin of the lady who brought it.

The moral is plain: Molded salads are best served in situations where they have little or no competition.

One reason is that many people don't trust molded salads, because of past experience. Like television, gelatin is too often a vehicle for limp leftovers that couldn't make it anywhere else.

Also, in a molded salad you'll often run across marshmallows, Brazil nuts, and similar goodies, that somehow escaped the dessert corral.

Another thing: to many people, anything molded tastes like junket. The gelatin always has a curiously gelatinous feel.

Yet, you keep on seeing so many molded salads around!

Well, it took me a long time to realize that the reason you do is that *the molded salad is easiest on the cook*. Only consider, for a moment, its advantages:

1. If you choose the right recipe, it's about as easy as a mud pie.

2. It's easy to carry somewhere else.

3. You can make it the day before. In fact, many of them unmold more easily and improve—not enough, but somewhat —if you do make them the day before. Or, say you want to get it out of the way before you head for the office or the laundromat. It's ready. No last-minute business with salad greens.

4. One molded salad serves many people, because they seldom go back for seconds.

5. If the mold and the plate are pretty, and if you garnish it with something attractive,[1] it will look as though you'd worked on it.

When you look at molded salads in this light, you can see that it doesn't much matter whether anyone really likes to eat them or not. So, without more ado, let's consider three. (There are 40,000 other aspic or molded-salad recipes in other cookbooks, of course. There is also an okay tomato aspic that comes in a can.)

---

[1] That is, something for contrapuntal effect with whatever is in the gelatin. Chopped fresh tomato or avocado, or canned mandarin-orange segments or grapefruit segments. Or something.

CHUTNEY ASPIC

8 servings

(To serve with chicken or turkey or anything curried. As a dressing you can mix equal parts of mayonnaise and sour cream, with lemon juice to taste.)

2 packages lime gelatin
1 cup hot water
1½ cups unsweetened pineapple juice
½ cup orange juice
2 small (8- or 9-ounce) cans crushed pineapple, drained
1 cup chutney (chopped a bit, if the chutney is chunky)

First oil a 6- or 8-cup mold thoroughly with salad oil.

Put the gelatin in a bowl, pour the hot water in and stir, then add everything else. Pour it into the mold and put it in the refrigerator.

(Most molds, by the way, have their capacities engraved on them somewhere. If yours doesn't, find out first how much it holds by filling it with measuring cupfuls of water—4 make a quart. Be sure to pour out the water before pouring the salad in.)

Unmolding the molded salad

Do it this way:

Set it momentarily in a larger pan of tepid water, then give it a gentle shake. Now hold the serving plate over the mold and turn the mold upside down.

Now peek. The salad will probably be right where it was. This is where the novice faces the stark certainty that she's up to here in trouble. But she isn't. She mustn't worry. She must think about something else, while she sets the mold in tepid water again for a tiny bit longer. (Or on a cloth wrung out in hot water.) This time it will slip out nicely, neat as a new-laid egg.

Once in a very long time, it may be necessary to slip a warmed knife blade between the mold and the gelatinous mass. But that happens only if you were a little too frugal in oiling the mold.

Now for

ANGOSTURA ASPIC

6-8 servings

Mix together in a saucepan

> 2 envelopes unflavored gelatin
> ½ cup sugar

and stir in

> 1 cup cold water.

Heat it gently till the gelatin dissolves. Then take it off the burner and add

> 2 tablespoons lemon or lime juice
> 2 cups grapefruit juice
> ½ cup sherry
> ½ teaspoon angostura bitters.

Pour it into a well-oiled ring mold—6-cup size—and put it in the refrigerator.

Now you must make a choice. Are you going to use

> a cup of grapefruit sections
> a cup of seedless grapes

as an ingredient? Or as a garnish?

If you decide on Ingredient, don't add it immediately, because it would sink. Wait a bit. Open the refrigerator in fifteen minutes or so and prod the aspic gently to see if it's started to set. Then close the door. Then open it and test it again and close it, and keep on doing this for a while, depending on the temperature of your refrigerator. This takes a good deal of nervous hanging around, which hardly seems worth it to me.

You can just put the fruit in the center of the ring mold when you serve it, and it will look very nice. Sliced avocado looks good with it and tastes good too.

There is also a school that feels it's all right if the fruit does sink. When you turn the mold over, the bottom of the thing is the top anyway.

While we're *en gelée* together, let's consider one other molded affair, which is a very pretty color.

SHIVERING ELIZABETH

> 1 package orange gelatin
> 2 small cans mandarin oranges (drained, but save the juice)
> 2 tablespoons lemon juice, plus enough of the mandarin juice you just saved to make a cupful
> 1 pint orange sherbet

Heat the juice, then pour it over the gelatin, and stir it till the gelatin is dissolved. Take it off the heat, cool it, and keep an eye on it, because it sets *fast*. Maybe ten minutes. When it starts to, add the sherbet and orange sections, stir it, pour it into a well-oiled 6- to 8-cup mold and put it away in the refrigerator.

On it you can serve

CHUTNEY SOUR CREAM DRESSING

> 1 cup sour cream
> ½ cup chopped chutney
> juice of ½ lemon or lime

Now we'll go on to happier things.

One of them is the fact that Ac'cent (MSG) heightens and improves the flavor of most salad dressings, just as it does nearly everything else. Yet few people, even the dedicated MSG group, think to use it there.

Another is the fact that you can make good Caesar salad without the last-minute raw-egg business.

READY CAESAR SALAD

(It's good without the anchovies, too; it's just a different salad then.)

Into a pint jar put
the juice of 1½ lemons
  (4 tablespoons)
¼ cup olive oil
½ teaspoon ground pepper
1 teaspoon Worcestershire
  sauce

½ teaspoon garlic powder
½ teaspoon salt
1 beaten egg
½ cup Parmesan cheese
4-6 anchovies, chopped, or
  more if you like them very
  much

Shake the jar with vigor, once you've put the things in and the lid on. Then keep it in the refrigerator till dinnertime. At serving time, pour it over romaine (because you want the salad to be dark green and crisp) and add croutons, say half a cupful to a cup.

A note about croutons: In another book I once wrote, I said that when you hate to cook, you'd much rather buy croutons than make them. This is, of course, true. But I've decided now that it is easier to make them than to eat the ones you can buy. Somewhere in North Philadelphia, I've heard, is a central vat of old sewing-machine oil which all the crouton people use to fry their bread cubes in. Every brand I've tried—and I don't give up easily on these things—is as bad as it's overpriced.

Therefore, inasmuch as croutons are important to the Ready Caesar Salad, I include here again the Crouton Rule:

> ¼ cup olive oil
> 4 slices of bread, diced
> 1 garlic clove, cut in half.

Put the olive oil in a skillet over low heat, add the garlic, and when the oil is hot, add the bread squares. Stir it so that each square is coated. Remove the garlic halves after a bit, and when the bread squares are nicely browned (which may not be longer than five minutes, so don't wander off), drain them on absorbent paper. They keep well in a covered jar in the refrigerator.

The next four salad recipes can be done ahead, too. Indeed, the first three should be (in that time of day you've chosen for doing your cooking—see page 33), keeping in mind how comforting it will be later, as you drag your wagon into the kitchen, to know your salad is all ready. Should you lose your impetus and not make it, you can still—at the last moment— simply slice the cucumbers and peppers as always and serve them with whatever dressing is around.

SIDE-DISH SALAD

4 servings

1 green pepper
2 cucumbers, unpeeled
some onion rings, if you like
1½ teaspoons salt

2 tablespoons vinegar
1 cup sour cream
paprika or coarse-ground
  pepper

Two or three hours or longer before serving, slice the pepper, onion, and cucumbers very thin. Put them in a bowl, sprinkle with salt, and refrigerate them. Mix the vinegar with the sour cream, too, so it will be ready.

Before dinner, drain the vegetables, stir them about in the dressing, and decorate with paprika or coarse-ground pepper.

GOOD SPINACH SALAD

6 servings

(*Spinach is sometimes a nice change from lettuce, and it is especially becoming to a pale dinner.*)

First, mix

2 tablespoons wine vinegar	1 teaspoon garlic powder
6 tablespoons olive oil	salt to taste.

Or, if you keep a bottle of vinegar-and-oil dressing around, use a half-cupful. Just be sure it's well garlicked.

Now hard-boil 3 eggs and fry 8 strips of bacon. Drain the bacon on paper towels. Wash a pound of spinach thoroughly, dry it, tear it in pieces, put it in a bowl, and refrigerate it.

When you're ready to serve dinner, chop the eggs and crumble the bacon into the bowl, then toss it all with the dressing. Parmesan cheese is good on this, and so are croutons, but neither is vital.

This next one uses up radishes and some of your canned beans.

ROSY RADISH SALAD

4-6 servings

Fry, drain, and crumble 4 slices of bacon.
Mix them with

a middle-sized chopped onion	⅛ teaspoon pepper
2 tablespoons vinegar	a sprinkle of Ac'cent (MSG)
1 tablespoon sugar	1-pound can of green beans,
½ teaspoon salt	drained
	1 cup of sliced radishes

Leave it in the refrigerator several hours so the flavors get friendly, then serve it on lettuce.

Finally, at the salad counter, here's one that's handy because it's also a dip if you want it to be. Increase the sour cream to make it dippable and skip the tomato shells—just use a finely chopped tomato.

GUACAMOLE TOMATOES

4 tomatoes hollowed out	a small chopped onion
(save the pulp)	1 tablespoon lemon juice
1 large ripe avocado	½ cup sour cream

Mash the avocado, then mix it with the tomato pulp and the rest. Spike it if you like with Tabasco, salt, and pepper. Stuff it into the tomatoes and serve it on lettuce.

". . . As for the foil-wrapped baked potato, sloshed with sour cream and laced with onions so that no trace of potato flavor remains, I give up. You find this culinary dead end everywhere, served with a proud flourish (and bits of bacon, if

*you don't watch out). They put foil around it to render the
jacket damp and soggy, which I guess is the way people like
it. I didn't come here to argue."*

—HERB CAEN

Though perhaps Herb Caen should howdy with Truman
Capote, back on page 21.

And now let's zero in on the swift little hot green vegetable,
which has a tendency to finish cooking faster than the rest of
the meal does.

There is a mystique, by the way, about serving hot things
smoking hot and cold things icy cold which is hard on the
tooth enamel, as well as on the people who are doing the
cooking.

It's a neat trick when you can do it because it makes things
taste a notch better. Plates you've chilled make a salad more
effective, somehow. And the reputation of many a steak
house has been built on the sizzle.

But sometimes—especially in the matter of hot food—the
food and the people don't synchronize. That's because real
life is different from gourmet-cookbook life.

In gourmet-cookbook life, there are no lumps or knobbly
places. But in real life, the clarion call to dinner is often the
signal for the man of the house to start taking apart his out-
board motor in the basement while the daughter of the house
disappears in a panic search for hair curlers. Chances are
good anyway that the people won't hit the table the same
minute the food does.

However, next to the family, vegetables are the stickiest
wickets, because so many of them take so little cooking. And
right here we must go back to the prime fact presented in
Chapter 1: *Few things cannot be interrupted while cooking.*
It's simply a matter of deciding who's in charge here—the
cook or the dinner.

Therefore, the thing to do, when you think of it, is to cook
a green vegetable a few minutes less than it's supposed to
be. (A minute-minder is handy here.) Then pull it off the
burner, remove the lid, so it won't steam, pour off the water,
if any, and add the butter and seasonings. You can reheat
it at any time in the butter, for another couple of minutes,
and it won't be overcooked.

Forward now to five swift vegetables with rather a company taste.

1. SWIFT MUSHROOM SPINACH

4 servings

Mix a can of undiluted condensed mushroom soup with a package of frozen cooked drained spinach. Add a teaspoon of vinegar. Heat it till it's hot.

Sliced water chestnuts or chopped walnuts would be good in this. Still, that's one more step, and it's good without it.

2. HOT CHERRY TOMATOES

5-6 servings

1 basket cherry tomatoes, stemmed
3 tablespoons butter
1 teaspoon chopped dried dill

Heat everything in a double boiler for fifteen minutes.

3. DELICATE ZUCCHINI

4-5 servings

5 or 6 zucchini squashes, grated on a coarse grater
¼ cup water
1 teaspoon onion flakes
½ cup Imo or yogurt

(Imo is a little like yogurt, and either one works fine here.)

Cook the squash in the water for five minutes. Drain it. STOP HERE, redrain and add everything else, plus a little butter, salt, and pepper. Then reheat it.

4. GUEST CHOKES

6 servings

(*You could serve these cold, too, as an upgraded pickle on a picnic.*)

First, simmer ½ cup of minced onion and a garlic clove in a little butter for five minutes. Take the garlic out and add

⅔ cup chicken stock
    (the bouillon-cube kind of powder)
2 15-ounce cans artichoke hearts, drained
3 tablespoons lemon juice
1½ teaspoons salt
1 teaspoon oregano.

Simmer it all with the lid on for another ten minutes. Just reheat and serve. Grated lemon rind would be a thoughtful note on top.

5. GUEST SPROUTS

5-6 servings

Cook two packages of frozen Brussels sprouts according to directions, and drain them.

In a little saucepan, heat

> 4 tablespoons butter
> 1 tablespoon prepared mustard
> 2 tablespoons lemon juice.[2]

Pour the sauce over the Brussels sprouts. STOP HERE. Heat it all together, then serve.

So here we are, as ready as we'll ever be to deal with the hot vegetable casserole.

The reason we must do so is this: The truculent cook, operating on a short culinary tether, never gets too far away from the chop, the steak, and the hamburger. And not only does a hot vegetable casserole round out that sort of meal in an authoritative way, but it also often enables her to dispense with something—a starch, a salad, or rolls.

That is what these five casseroles do. And another big point: They all bake in a 325° oven. That means that if you roast beef at 325° for twenty minutes to the pound, you can bake the vegetables right along with it.

1. EXTRAORDINARILY GOOD EGGPLANT

6 servings

> 1 eggplant, unpeeled
> 2 chopped onions
> 4 tablespoons butter
> 1 can smoked oysters, coarsely chopped
> ⅔ cup crushed Ritz crackers (plain or cheese)

Cut the eggplant into small pieces and simmer them, covered, in salted water till they're tender—about ten minutes. With your other hand sauté the chopped onions in the butter till they're tender, too.

Drain the eggplant thoroughly in a colander, pressing it with paper towels to dry it thoroughly. Then mix together

[2] It's hard to think of a vegetable, by the way, that isn't the better for a squirt of it, except maybe turnips and baked beans. So that's a good easy thing to keep in mind, just as some reconstituted lemon juice is a good thing to keep in the refrigerator (see page 50). The purists don't regard it too highly, but it's a great deal better than no lemon at all. It's also stronger than the garden kind, so go easy.

everything except half the cracker crumbs, and put it in a casserole dish. Put the rest of the crumbs on top. STOP HERE. Bake for thirty-five minutes at 325°.

2. CORN CHIP CASSEROLE

6 servings

(A nice idea with chicken, ham, hamburgers)

Sauté

> ¼ cup sliced green onions
> ¾ cup sliced celery

in

> 1 tablespoon butter

till they're tender.

Then mix

> 2 slightly beaten eggs
> ⅓ cup milk
> ½ teaspoon crumbled oregano
> ¼ teaspoon salt
> 1 17-ounce can cream-style corn (this is Del
>   Monte's recipe, so I use their brand,
>   which seems only right).

Add the cooked onions and celery to the second mixture, and have 6 ounces of corn chips ready as well as ¼ pound of grated yellow cheese.

In a casserole dish, layer the corn mixture, the chips, and the cheese till you run out of material, ending—if you can— with the chips. STOP HERE. Bake at 325° for forty minutes, uncovered.

3. JOAN'S CONTRIBUTION

6-8 servings

(This includes—as you will see—five vegetables, and it's good anyway.)

1 package frozen chopped spinach	½ teaspoon salt
	¼ teaspoon tarragon
1 package frozen chopped broccoli	¼ teaspoon pepper
(or 2 packages of either)	some French-fried onion rings
	½ cup grated yellow cheese
1 can condensed mushroom or celery soup	2 middle-sized tomatoes, peeled and quartered

Cook the spinach and the broccoli a little less than the box says you're supposed to, adding a tablespoon of vinegar to each.

Add the seasonings to the soup, then fold in the drained

spinach and broccoli. Pour it into a flattish buttered baking tin, and arrange the onions and tomatoes on top. Sprinkle on the cheese. STOP HERE. Bake it at 325° for thirty-five minutes, or 250° for forty-five minutes, whichever is handier.

N.B. You can double this easily should you need to. If you do, make it one can of mushroom soup *and* a can of celery.

4. CHEESE CELERY SPECIAL

4-5 servings
(*A good way to use up the large ungainly stalks*)

Cook 4 cups of coarsely chopped celery in water till it's tender but crisp. Drain it.

Then sauté

¼ cup chopped onion
1 chopped green pepper

in 2 tablespoons of butter. Into this, stir

about 4 ounces blue cheese
½ cup heavy cream.

Now add the drained celery, put it all in a baking dish, and cover with

1 cup of crumbs.

The crumb topping is better if you use coarse crumbs fried in a tablespoon of butter. But those out of a box are all right dotted with butter. STOP HERE.

Heat it through, about fifteen minutes, in a 325° oven.

5. GREEN-BEAN CASSEROLE

6-8 servings
(*I think a polite-tasting canned-bean recipe is handy to have.*)

2 cans green beans, drained (or an equal amount of any other kind, but canned is easiest)
¼ cup salad oil
2 medium chopped onions
a few parsley sprigs (or a teaspoon of dried)
1 teaspoon garlic powder
¼ cup cottage cheese
½ cup grated Cheddar cheese
4 eggs, slightly beaten
1 teaspoon salt
dash of pepper
1 cup of soft bread crumbs

Sauté the chopped onions in the salad oil till they're tender. Then add everything but the beans and stir it.

In a greased casserole dish, layer this mixture with the beans, trying to end up with the cheese mixture, though the sky won't fall if you don't. STOP HERE. Bake it, uncovered, for thirty minutes at 325°.

Finally, to taper off, here are two generalized approaches to the vegetable that seem to improve most of them.

The first is

ALL-AROUND CRUMB TOPPING

Fry a cup of rather coarse bread crumbs in ¼ pound of butter till they're brown. Sprinkle them on hot precooked salted-and-peppered asparagus, string beans, broccoli, cauliflower. . . .

If you wanted to sprinkle Parmesan cheese on top of that, and put the dish under the broiler for a minute, you could. But you're not supposed to if there's cheese elsewhere in the dinner, for that would be a sort of culinary stutter. Anyway, we must cut corners where we can.

The other one is

BLENDER HOLLANDAISE

(*Hollandaise isn't the ugly word it used to be if you have a blender, though if you don't, make the sauce on page 116. However, the blender kind seems perfectly safe, for anybody. This recipe is from* The Blender Cookbook, *by Ann Seranne and Eileen Gaden,[3] and I'm bound to admit it works beautifully.*)

Heat slowly ¼ pound of butter in a saucepan till it bubbles. But don't let it brown.

At the same time, in your blender jar put

3 egg yolks	¼ teaspoon salt
2 tablespoons lemon juice	pinch of cayenne pepper.

Cover the container and turn motor on low speed. Immediately remove the cover and pour in the hot butter in a steady stream. When all the butter is added, turn off the motor. This makes ¾ of a cupful, enough for four or five people.

And so, on those rare occasions when one feels like doing anything to a vegetable besides buttering and salting and peppering it, these are all things to consider. Or, at any rate, you might drop them into an 8-cup mold and see if they jell.

CHAPTER 8

Knowledgeable People,
Stealing from

I SEEN HER WHEN SHE DONE IT
BUT I NEVER LEFT ON

"He ought to be good, he's using my act."
—FRED ALLEN

I believe that the truly dedicated cook has food on her mind, or at least on the periphery of it, at all times. As a poet unconsciously earmarks a word that rhymes handily with another, or as a painter mentally notes a tint of a shade of a color that spells Dawn, so the food-minded person sniffs an out-of-the-way herb, like costmary, and thinks in a flash, *Braised moose hocks!*

But the rest of us are not similarly talented. While our reflexes are dependable—if you say Fried Chicken, we think Mashed Potatoes; say Baked Beans, we think Brown Bread—

they're hardly inspired. If we get a sniff of costmary, we'll only think, with mild surprise, *For goodness' sake*.

For this reason it is important to observe the little ways of these knowledgeable cooks. It is equally important, sometimes, not to let them know you're observing them, for some are absolute stinkers when it comes to sharing the wealth. Ask one for that soufflé recipe she's so proud of, and chances are you'll get it without the eggs. But one must be tolerant. Perhaps this recipe is the brightest plume on her beanie, and you wouldn't want to take it away from her, especially since you'd end up with a mess.

Not that all of them are this way, by any means. Indeed, some are almost too generous with their inspirations. Should you be grocery shopping with one and you pause at the halibut, she's apt to explode with something like, "I make the most marvelous whipped-cream–cucumber sauce for my baked halibut!"

That's a clear cue, of course, to ask for the recipe. But you're not *obliged* to. You may answer, simply, "Do you?" and hang onto your original notion of serving it pan fried and plain as the good Lord grew it.

One thing, though: Should a knowledgeable cook ever erupt like this with a recipe you happen to want, it is important to *write it down*. Where food is concerned, unwilling cooks have the attention span of a four-year-old and should never trust to memory.

This happened to me once with a salad—a devastatingly delicious *new* kind (my friend said) and a real break-through on the green salad front. She gave me the recipe, which I didn't write down, and accordingly I forgot the brown sugar and the tarragon. It didn't amount to shucks.

However, when I ate it at her house, I discovered that it definitely does, when you make it right. So I want to include it here.

BREAK-THROUGH SALAD

6 servings

Your vegetables consist of
  2 medium green peppers, thinly sliced in strips
  ½ cup coarsely chopped parsley
  2 cups coarsely chopped endive or chicory
  3 medium tomatoes cut in eighths
  2 tablespoons chopped chives (or dried minced green onion)

2 tablespoons minced black olives (not strictly necessary
but pretty).
Then mix together
¼ cup water
½ cup tarragon vinegar
½ teaspoon salt
1½ tablespoons lemon juice
1 tablespoon brown sugar.

Pour this over the vegetables and let it wait in the refrigerator till serving time. Then put a good tablespoon of sour
cream on each serving.

Of course, it isn't merely recipes that these people con-
tribute. They have all sorts of wee wisdoms, like the fact that
if you keep Brazil nuts in the freezer overnight, they'll crack
beautifully and with ease. And they also know efficient ways
of doing things, some of which can be most helpful. Take,
for example, the Rule of Thumb and Forefinger.

A knowledgeable French-schooled cook on television stresses the convenience of knowing how much salt (and so forth)
you can take in a pinch. Then you needn't mess up measuring spoons for it.

I've found my own capacity to be a scant one-eighth teaspoon.[1] To get a teaspoonful, doing that eight times is more
trouble than measuring. But it's handy for smaller quantities.

Also, I've found that it helps in casual recipes to be able
to gauge, by eye, a half-cupful of chopped or grated cheese
or celery and so on. Once you've shaped a half-cupful of it
into a small funeral mound and stared at it hard, you can
gauge it from then on, at least well enough for stews, salads,
toppings, casseroles . . . though of course you wouldn't do
this for mousses or other precision affairs, or you would find
yourself up the old crick.

Then consider the matter of leftover chicken. Recipes that
begin with "Take 2 cups of leftover chicken" have little
allure, because there's seldom any left over except for a wing
and a neck, and you're not about to roast or fry one. The
tendency is to skip it.

I won't soon forget the day I saw a friend of mine mat-
ter-of-factly start simmering some frozen chicken thighs in a
little water with a chicken bouillon cube, and then, for about

[1] I customarily use a thumb-and-two-finger pinch. A one-finger
pinch retrieves slightly less.

twenty-five minutes, go and do something else. She was going to use them that night in a casserole; and being the fore-sighted little thing that she is, she probably froze the broth to use later for diluting a can of soup.

This is the sort of beautiful, simple thing that natural cooks do naturally, but unnatural cooks don't think of. Even when they hear about it, their strong tendency is to skip it. Still, it is a good thing to know.

At a dinner party once, I ate a small broiled *filet mignon* on a slice of grilled eggplant that had been dipped in egg and oregano-spiked crumbs. It was quite good and made the steak seem bigger.

I asked my hostess, a real swinger, if she'd thought it up. She said, No, that it was her habit to keep her little red eyes open, and that's what *her* hostess had served the previous Saturday night. Thus does information get around.

And once I saw a weekend hostess of mine spread prepared mustard-horseradish and plenty of pepper all over a pork roast before she cooked it. This impressed me considerably, and so did the way it tasted later. The treatment seemed to cut the richness.

Then there was the time I saw a lady pour off the juice from a brand-new bottle of olives and cover them with olive oil. That way, she said, they don't get moldy. I thought this was shrewd of her, because it also provided a small reserve of olive oil, like a dime in your pants pocket.

As a matter of fact, a cook needn't be expert to be worth stealing from. Once, I saw the worst cook I ever met (her husband is philosophic about it, and they dine out a great deal) use a cheese grater to remove the charred part from the burned toast. This could be a handy little technique, at the end of a loaf.

However, the two main areas in which observation, or stealing, has been of most value to me are those of The Tea and The Lunch.

The tea

As James Thurber has put it so nicely, "There are rules and rites and rituals, older than the sound of bells and snow on mountains."

These three R's underlie the social tea, consisting mainly

—as it does—of women standing about and saying things they don't mean[2] while eating things they don't want.

Most of these rules, rites, and rituals are in any big fat cookbook. The main thing to remember is that if you have a number of small pale objects around on pretty plates, you probably have a good tea going. The fact that they look a little anemic and unnecessary doesn't mean that you're unimaginative; only correct.

When you don't like to cook, you're undoubtedly talented and energetic in other ways, one of which is probably avoiding teas, either going to them or giving them. The one possible peril is a committee you might find yourself on—a committee of an organization given to good works and large teas, to which each member is expected to bring something rather devastating in the line of tea sandwiches.

Someone has already volunteered, probably, her marvelous homemade thin-brown-bread-and-butter sandwiches. Or her marvelous homemade thin-orange-bread-and-butter sandwiches. You can't say she's fibbing, because she's going to make the sandwiches, all right—spread and trim them. But chances are good she'll buy the bread from a good bakery or small gourmet shop. These places often have a specialty bread that's better than most amateurs can make.

As a general thing, you can volunteer whichever kind she didn't.

Therefore, these three tea-sandwich rules are offered only as one would offer a bottle of poison-ivy lotion, in the hope that it won't be necessary.

(Teacakes or cookies are no problem, because you can usually buy good ones. And if you can't, the Danish Almond Sheet on page 141 is a fairly simple solution.)

For all these sandwiches, cream the butter first.

CUCUMBER DILLWICHES

Flatten thin-sliced white bread with a rolling pin (which is a good idea for any tea sandwich) and cut it in rounds with a biscuit cutter. Unless you have square cucumbers.

On each, spread butter. Put a thin slice of peeled cucumber on the butter, sprinkle fresh chopped dill or the dried kind on the cucumber. Then put another buttered bread

---

[2] This is largely true of the Cocktail Party as well, except that there is sometimes more *veritas* in the *vino*.

round on the top. That's all, but they have a very nice lady-like look.

ALMOND CHICKWICHES

Spread bread slices with softened butter. (You cut and trim these later.)

For the filling, mix

1 can minced chicken
1 small jar pimento pieces, drained and chopped
½ cup chopped salted almonds
¼ cup mayonnaise

1 teaspoon minced chives (or chopped green onion tops)
1 tablespoon parsley, chopped
2 or 3 drops angostura bitters, if you like.

Spread it on half the bread slices, put the other buttered bread slices on top, trim the crusts, and cut each sandwich into 4 small squares or 4 small triangles.

OPEN FACEWICHES

Butter flattened bread slices. Spread each with a mixture of

8 ounces cream cheese, softened and well blended with
3 tablespoons finely chopped chutney
2 tablespoons finely chopped preserved ginger
¼ cup grated coconut
½ teaspoon curry powder.

Now—a mussy operation, this—trim the crusts off and cut each slice into three strips. Wash hands when done.

The lunch

This is a more rewarding area of research, because most ideas you pilfer can be used for other occasions, too.

The best lunch I've been to in years was basically ham and eggs and champagne. It had two big advantages: It was a cinch for the hostess, and the men liked it as well as the women.

The menu was

Melon Balls
Ham and Eggs in Individual Baking Dishes
Orange Walnut Muffins
Champagne

THE HAM AND EGGS

4 servings

Put a slice of boiled or baked ham in each of 4 shallow baking dishes. Break two eggs—rather carefully—over it in each. Then make a sauce:

Melt ¼ cup of butter, stir in ¼ cup of flour, add 1 cup of milk and ½ cup of chicken stock. (Bouillon-cube stock does fine.) Cook till it's thickened, then salt and pepper it, and add ½ cup of vermouth.

Pour the sauce over the eggs and sprinkle it with grated yellow cheese or Romano or Parmesan. STOP HERE (and if you've done this early, better refrigerate it because of the eggs).

Bake the little dishes at 400° for ten to fifteen minutes.

THE MUFFINS

Use a package of orange-muffin mix and add a half-cupful of chopped walnuts or pecans. They can bake right along with the ham and eggs.

THE MELON BALLS

Use, preferably, fresh, for they're much better than frozen. But they needn't be balls; they could be chunks. Or strips. Or just plain melon.

Our hostess told me later that she had everything ready to put in the oven or take out of the refrigerator by 11:00 A.M. And indeed, I noticed that she was relaxed enough to enjoy the champagne quite as much as the rest of us.

One other sort of lunch, I've noticed, seems equally easy on the person who is giving it. This is the Soup-with-Something Lunch. The soup is ready on the back of the stove; and the Something (dessert, or French loaf, or sandwiches) needs only putting in the oven or on the table, as the case may be.

It is best to have a hard-to-analyze soup. I've noticed that the knowledgeable hostess seldom serves anything you have a freezer full of yourself, or, at least if she does, you don't recognize it. (And in any case, the knowledgeable guest would never beam and say, "I simply *adore* Murgatroyd's Chowder; we have it all the time at home!" for this would say volumes about her upbringing, or downbringing.)

This is why you combine soups, or doctor them conscientiously. However, this must be tempered with sense. If you're going to take half an hour out of your life to make Picayune Pecan Pie (page 147), your guests could get along nicely with plain frozen vegetable soup, which is excellent as is. You could add some fresh chopped cucumber to it at the last minute if you wanted to, but you certainly wouldn't have to.

The next five recipes include three easy and almost unrecognizable soups and two moderately interesting sandwiches.

SUDDEN SOUP

4 *servings*

(*Light, somewhat exotic, and good with the Chutney Loaf or the Voodoo Sandwiches*)

Boil together till it's reduced about half
    4 cans chicken broth
    1 cup tomato juice
    salt and pepper.

Then add a dash of sugar, the grated rind of half an orange, and ¼ cup of dry vermouth. STOP HERE. Heat it again and serve.

PHILOSOPHER'S CHOWDER

4-6 *servings*

(*Rather pretty, and good with a fruit dessert*)

Cook a package of frozen chopped spinach in the least possible water. Drain it.[3] Then put it in the blender with 2 cans of minced clams, including the juice, for seven or eight seconds, till it's thoroughly puréed.

Then pour it into a saucepan and add 2 cups of light cream (or 2 cups of whole milk with a walnut-size chunk of butter) and bring it to just below a boil. Season it with salt, pepper, and a spatter of nutmeg. Good cold, too.

ACAPULCO BEAN SOUP

4 *servings*

(*Actually, this is recognizable and won't fool anybody. But*

---

[3] Another thing I've noticed is that expert cooks seem to drain their spinach very hard, especially when it's going into a casserole. They practically stamp on it to get all the water out. It isn't all that important in soup though.

*it's pleasantly picturesque, and with plenty of corn chips
and a melon, it's an attractive lunch.*)

Combine

2 cans concentrated black bean soup	2 teaspoons chili powder
	½ teaspoon dried oregano
2 soup cans water	2 tablespoons sherry.

Simmer it ten minutes. Then top it with chopped green
onions and coarsely grated yellow cheese, preferably Cheddar.

VOODOO SANDWICHES

8-10 *servings*

(*A two-stage operation—the onions need fixing the day before. It all adds up to a rather subtle-tasting sandwich that's
good with the Philosopher's Chowder, say, or two canned
soups combined: cream of tomato with cream of celery, or
cream of mushroom with cream of oyster. They're good
hearty canapés, too.*)

The day before, slice 2 mild medium white onions into a
deep bowl. Bring a cup of water and half a cup of sugar to
a boil and pour it over them. Now apply a layer of ice cubes
and put the bowl in the refrigerator.

Next day, drain the onion slices and dry them between
paper towels. Then mix

1 cup mayonnaise
½ teaspoon dry mustard
1 teaspoon lemon juice.

Spread good white bread with it, using the onion slices
for filling, with a good sprinkle of salt and coarse-ground
pepper. Trim the crusts, then cut into 4 triangles. Spread
the edges with mayonnaise and dip the edges in chopped
parsley (you'll need about a cupful).

Then refrigerate them till lunchtime.

A good thing to know about onions, by the way, is how
to make a strong harsh onion more presentable. You slice
it thinly and pour boiling water on the slices. Then drain
and chill them, and they'll emerge sweeter as well as crisper.

HOT CHUTNEY LOAF

makes 6 sandwiches

(*A matter of slicing a French loaf and reassembling it*)

Cut a small loaf of French bread into 12 slices.

Mix a small can of deviled ham with ¼ cupful of chutney. Spread this on half the slices, sharp Cheddar on the other half. Put a tomato slice between each two, then re-form the sandwiches into a loaf, wrap it in aluminum foil, and bake it at 425° for about fifteen minutes.

The hostess from whom I liberated this recipe served Daiquiris first and a fresh fruit salad with the loaf. I thought it all added up nicely.

One other point: Knowledgeable cooks are often comforting as well as informative.

For example, I once saw one become annoyed at the way her eggs poached, or didn't—the whites disintegrating into ectoplasmic wisps. She was annoyed not at herself but at her grocer, for selling her stale eggs, which, she said, was the reason for their poor performance. I was glad to learn this. Knowing something isn't your fault can improve the morale if not the meal.

Or take Hollandaise. As indicated earlier, preoccupied cooks find Hollandaise about as dependable as false eyelashes in a wind tunnel, and the blender type (page 106) is no help if you haven't a blender. I was delighted to learn from a good-cooking friend of mine about an absent-minded sour-cream dressing, affectionately known as

HUNTLEY-BRINKLEY HOLLANDAISE

(*To make before settling down with a highball before dinner to watch the news*)

See to it that the water in the bottom of the double boiler is definitely below boiling. Just good and hot. In the top, mix

> 4 egg yolks
> 1 cup dairy sour cream
> 1 tablespoon lemon juice
> dash of hot pepper sauce
> ½ teaspoon salt.

Then go away. It doesn't much matter when you come back . . . one hour, two hours. Stir it thoroughly then, and it will be absolutely lovely on the fish. Or the broccoli. Or the asparagus . . .

Clearly, then, these knowledgeable cooks can be of assistance. They do know some tidy little ways of doing things, as well as some tidy little things to do.

But all this can be deceptive. You find yourself beginning to trust them. Until they come up, one day, with something like, "It's no trouble at all to poach a bit of sole in wine, then garnish it with whole cooked shrimp to serve as a first course and show off your pretty fish forks!"

Statements like this make you realize that some of these people have a great respect for the truth—in fact, too much respect to use it just any old time.

CHAPTER 9

Meal, End of the

IRISH COFFEE REVISITED

"My! I hope you didn't go to a lot of trouble!"
—CHRISTINE FREDERICK

It is a sorely distressful thing when you are Irish to admit that there is another side to a question. This is particularly true when it is a question of Irish Coffee.[1] Even though Irish Coffee was invented by an Italian bartender in San Francisco, ancestral honor seems somehow involved.

[1] IRISH COFFEE: Put 1½ ounces of Irish whisky into a stemmed glass. Add 1½ teaspoons of granulated sugar. Add 1½ teaspoons of instant coffee. Fill to within half an inch of the brim with hot water and stir. Now, on top, float whipped cream, which should be thick but not stiff. (½ cup of cream, before whipping, is about right for 4 Irish Coffees.) (From *The I Hate to Cook Book.*)

It is with embarrassed reluctance, therefore, that I revise an original glowing estimate of mine concerning Irish Coffee as a dinner-party dessert. Contrary to my earlier recommendations, it doesn't solve every problem.

Indeed, it can create some. For one, when you bring on the Irish Coffee, an occasional guest will think happily that the cocktail hour is beginning all over again, and he may dig in for the night. For another, some people don't drink.

But its biggest drawback is its extremely last-minute preparation, which is the last thing you need. When you finally get the evening on a downhill pull, you want to keep it that way.

All the recipes in this chapter—with one great awkward exception—enable you to do just that. They can all be made in advance. This chapter will thus contain no STOP HERES.

How to bypass pastry

Some people, so they tell me, can't make good pastry. I see no reason to doubt them. Some people can't keep their eyes open under water, either, and some people can't remember their zip codes, and that is simply the way it is. We all have our mental blocks to play with.

But there are several ways around this one.

One is the pastry mix. There are two kinds, though many brands, that I know of: the kind that's in sticks and the kind that isn't. The stick kind is ever so slightly easier, or so it seems to me.

Most of them make an adequate pie shell, better than mediocre though not so good as the best. It will be a perfectly all-right pie if one's determination holds through the filling.

Then there is the crumb crust with no topping, or with a crumb-sugar topping.

Still another way of side-stepping pastry is the *torte,* which can't technically be considered a pie. Still, it is pie-shaped, and the unwilling pie-maker isn't about to split hairs.

THE CRUMB CRUST

A good basic rule is

1½ cups gingersnap crumbs

¼ cup confectioners' sugar (though this isn't vital, and if the filling is to be quite rich, skip it)

6 tablespoons melted butter.

Mix it well and pat it into a pie pan. Don't try to flute it or bring it up over the rim of the pan. It would crumble when you cut into it, because that's the way the gingersnaps.

Then chill it for an hour or so before you fill it. Or bake it at 375° for fifteen minutes.

Instead of gingersnap crumbs you can use chocolate-cookie crumbs. (A good switch is 17 Hydrox cookies and 4 tablespoons of melted butter.)

Or you can use graham crackers or vanilla wafers. In fact, you can use nearly any sort of crisp plain cookie or assortment of them. Sometimes the family doesn't eat the last few in a package, and you can put these in the blender or under the rolling pin in waxed paper, then into the jar that houses your sweet-crumb collection (not the jar on page 65). It's rather like the old soup kettle on the back of the stove, with something new periodically added. This can make for an interesting pie shell.

As to what you put in it, there are some packaged mixes that make an okay everyday pie. It won't look too packaged with some lemon rind or orange rind or chopped ginger sprinkled on a fruit-pudding type, or grated bitter chocolate on a chocolate-pudding type. Or you can save some of the crumbs and sprinkle them on top.

Another good simple way to use a crumb crust is for a

CHILLY CHOCOLATE PIE

Blend for a minute, with a mixer or in a blender
    1 package instant vanilla pudding
    1 package instant chocolate pudding
    1½ cups milk.
Now add 1 pint of softened vanilla ice cream and a teaspoon of instant coffee. Mix it in. Pour it into the crumb crust, chill it, and grate bitter chocolate on top.

Then there is the matter of TOPPINGS, which bypass a top crust entirely, whatever the bottom one is.

For instance, you can make a very good French-type fruit pie like this:

Have a crumb crust ready.
In it, lay 6 sliced apples—and pears work exactly as well, if not better—mixed with

                       ½ cup sugar
                       1 teaspoon lemon rind
                       3 tablespoons lemon juice.
Now sprinkle the slices with a mixture of
½ cup flour   ½ teaspoon cinnamon
½ cup sugar   ¼ teaspoon mace
½ teaspoon ginger   ⅓ cup butter
   Bake it at 400° for forty-five minutes.

As anyone can see, this is easier and neater than rolling out
a piecrust.

Or skip the crumb or pastry shell altogether and make a

BROWN-SUGAR APPLE PIE

   Grease a pie plate, then peel and slice 6 apples. Put a layer
of slices in the pie plate, sprinkle with sugar, cinnamon, and
dots of butter. Stay with it till the apple slices are all in.
   To top it, blend
                       ½ cup brown sugar
                       ½ cup butter
                       1 cup flour
and flatten little dabs of this into crude circles (because it's
really too sticky to roll out). Arrange these in some casual
fashion on top of the apples, then bake at 350° for about half
an hour, or till the apples are soft.
   If any is left, you can reheat it next day to serve in pudding dishes, with cream or ice cream.

And finally, in the pie-shaped department, we come to a

NICE SIMPLE TORTE

   Beat three egg whites good and stiff. Gradually add 1 cup
of sugar and ½ teaspoon of baking powder.
   Now fold in 1 cup of chopped walnuts, filberts, or pecans,
and 11 2-inch graham crackers, well crushed. Pour it into a
well-greased pie pan and bake it at 350° for half an hour.
   When it is cool, cover it with ½ pint of whipping cream,
whipped with ½ teaspoon of vanilla, no sugar. It's a nice
touch, though, to spread a little jam on it, any sort, before
the whipped cream. Refrigerate it for three or four hours before you need it.

This brings us, as so many things do, to the matter of how to employ the leftover egg yolks.

In the Forgotten Meringue (page 125) everything comes out even and everyone lives happily ever after. But this is rare. If you don't need Hollandaise—and if you do, check pages 106 and 116—the sensible solution is to pretend the yolks were part of the shell and drop them down the sink. When you don't do this, when, in a splendid out-of-character moment, you cover the yolks with water to preserve them, and set them in the refrigerator, it only ages them, and they don't get used anyway. You made that *torte*, remember, and there is nothing you're about to make for a while that requires three egg yolks. Or, to put it another way, there is nothing you're about to make for a while.

Therefore, the pot-de-chocolat egg-yolk recipe we're coming to next doesn't refer to those same egg yolks, less one. These are different eggs and this time you throw away the whites. Though egg whites are easier to use up than yolks—for meringues, soufflés, chops before breading them, and so forth—you never seem to be doing those things when leftover egg whites are around. So it's best to dispose of them, else you've excess baggage on your conscience and in the refrigerator.

1. POT-DE-CHOCOLAT

6-7 servings

(*Most people like chocolate, and this recipe—from a blender booklet I'd gladly credit if I knew which one it was—is a good, velvety affair. It's also the first of five desserts that are much easier than they taste and have more status than pie.*)

Into the blender bowl put

    1 cup semisweet chocolate chips

    1¼ cups scalded[2] light cream (coffee cream)

    2 egg yolks

    3 tablespoons brandy (or rum)

Turn the switch to high speed and blend it till the racket stops. Pour it into any small pretty cups—Japanese teacups or demitasse cups—something small, because it's rich. Chill them about three hours.

---

[2] Heat it till just below boiling.

2. POT-DE-STRAWBERRY

6-8 *servings*

1 package lemon-flavor gelatin
1 cup hot water
1 10-ounce package frozen strawberries,
 somewhat thawed
1 cup heavy cream

Put the gelatin into the blender bowl and add the water. Cover it and blend it for about fifteen seconds. (You could use your egg beater or electric mixer, if you haven't a blender, but you'd have to press the strawberries through a sieve, which is an awful nuisance, and you'd do better to make something else.)

Add the strawberries, blend another five seconds or so, and set the bowl in the refrigerator for ten minutes. It should start to thicken by then. Add ¾ of the cream, unwhipped, and blend just a few seconds to mix it.

Pour it into those same charming little cups mentioned earlier, assuming they're empty again, and chill them several hours. Whip the remaining ¼ cup of cream to top it with. Chopped almonds are pretty on top of that.

That recipe has the big advantage of calling for frozen strawberries, and so does this one.

3. STRAWBERRIES MARY

(*You may have noticed that chefs and other experts like to name dishes after girls, much as the weatherman names his hurricanes: Potatoes Anna, Poires Hélène, Strawberries Susan. These are all gourmese for Anna's Potatoes and Helen's Pears and Susan's Strawberries. This recipe is called Strawberries Mary because it is the way Mary adapted Strawberries Susan, a famous fresh fruit recipe, to wintertime use.*)

2 or 3 bananas
1 tablespoon lemon juice
1 package frozen strawberries,
 partially thawed
3 tablespoons strawberry jam
5 macaroons, almond or
 coconut
½ cup whipping cream
slivered toasted almonds

Slice the bananas into a serving bowl. Sprinkle with the lemon juice, then add the strawberries mixed with the jam. Next come the macaroons, crumbled. Cover it all with the cream, whipped and slightly sweetened. Chill it an hour or so before you serve it with the almonds on top.

4. LONDON TRIFLE
(Note breath-taking simplicity here)

5-6 *servings*

    1 cup yogurt
    1 cup marmalade

Mix them up. Then taste. Maybe you'll want more yogurt. Or marmalade. Spoon it into sherbet glasses, grate some orange rind on top, and chill it a bit.

5. JULY COMPOTE

(Pretty, and easy, with the additional virtue of calling for bourbon, which one generally has around, instead of cognac, which one hasn't.)

All together now bring to a boil
    1 cup water
    1 cup sugar
    1 tablespoon bourbon
    grated rind of a big orange.

While it's still warm, pour it over
    3 big peaches, peeled, pitted, and sliced
    5 ripe plums, any kind, quartered and pitted
    1 cup seedless grapes.

Chill several hours. This looks best in a glass bowl.

And now for four clichés.

These are the dogged little recipes that keep appearing through the generations and disappearing and reappearing, like kneecaps in the fashion picture, or dining rooms in houses.

I believe this tenacity indicates certain quiet strengths: that people like them, and that they're easy to make. So I thought it might be comfortable to group the four here, as insurance against the next time they vanish around the bend.

1. VELVET LIME PIE

Have a pie shell ready, pastry or crumb.
For the filling you need
    1 can sweetened condensed milk
    1/3 cup fresh lime juice
    3 eggs.

First separate the eggs and beat the yolks. Mix them with the milk and lime juice, then whip the egg whites till they're stiff and fold them in. Pour it in a pie shell and bake for ten minutes at 250°. Chill it a while.

This is especially good topped with faintly sweetened whipped cream spiked with rum.

Also, right along with the Alamo, we must remember

2. FORGOTTEN MERINGUE

(*This is that well-adjusted recipe mentioned earlier that neatly uses up the eggs.*)

First, set the oven at 400°. Then beat 5 egg whites till they're foamy (and this time don't throw away the yolks). Add

    ¼ teaspoon salt
    ½ teaspoon cream of tartar

and this time keep on beating till they stand in limp peaks. Then, very gradually, add

    1½ cups sugar

and keep on beating till they're very stiff indeed.

Grease and flour a 9-inch pie plate, and spread the meringue in it, scooping it out of the middle and piling it a bit around the sides to form a shell. Put it in the 400° oven, turn the heat off immediately, and DON'T LOOK IN FOR 5 HOURS. Or overnight.

It's easiest and very good to fill this with slightly sweetened fresh fruit topped with sour cream. But to use up the 5 egg yolks, you can make a

5-EGG-YOLK LEMON FILLING

Beat the yolks, and gradually add

    ½ cup sugar.

Then blend in

    4 tablespoons lemon juice
    grated rind of a lemon

Stir this constantly over boiling water (in your double boiler) for six or seven minutes. Now whip

    1 cup of whipping cream

and spread half of it over the meringue. Then pour in the lemon mixture, top with the rest of the whipped cream, and refrigerate it. You can do the whole works the day before, because it keeps well.

One of the fast clichés is

3. 6-MINUTE CHEESECAKE

(*But I don't believe the optimist who named it allowed for the crumb crust or the baking time.*)

Have a crumb crust ready and set the oven at 325°.
Cream

>   2 small packages softened cream cheese
>   ½ cup sugar
>   ½ teaspoon vanilla
>   1 slightly beaten egg.

Put it in a crumb crust and bake it twenty minutes. Hike the oven up to 450°, spread a cup of sour cream all over the top of the pie, sprinkle a tablespoon of sugar on that, and bake it for five minutes. Then chill it.

This is complete as is, but it's good with fresh berries and fruit, too.

The last of the old faithfuls is

4. HOT ORANGE PUFF

4 servings

(*This one seems to surface every ten years or so wearing a different name. It's known as Marmalade Soufflé, too, as well as—I'm sorry to say—Fluffy Duffy. It is, by the way, the one big awkward exception, mentioned earlier, that you can't make well in advance. Worse still, it needs a sauce. Still, a non-cook I know swears by it.*)

>   4 egg whites
>   ¼ cup sugar
>   ¼ cup marmalade

Beat the whites till they're stiff, add the sugar, then the marmalade. Butter the top part of a double boiler. Pour the mixture in, sprinkle it lightly with sugar, then put on the lid. You're not supposed to sneak a look or cop a feel, though I did once and it didn't make any difference.

Cook it for an hour, the water simmering. Presumably you're at dinner now, and the puff will be ready for you when you're ready for it.

THE ORANGE PUFF'S VERY O

(*I suppose the other recipe calls it Fl*

Any time before dinner, beat 2 egg yo
½ cup of sugar. Flavor it with whatever gr   -a
tablespoon of rum, brandy, sherry. Or use vanilla.

Just before serving time, whip ¾ cup of cream till   ff
and fold it into the egg-and-sugar business. This make a
pourable sauce. Don't expect it to stand around in peaks.

I think softened vanilla ice cream blended with brandy
would be good with this, too.

Speaking of which, I know an enthusiastic cook who has
relied for years on vanilla ice cream plus a blender for desserts, and she still hasn't worked her way through all the
possible combinations.

When I saw her last, she had gone through fresh, canned,
and frozen fruits, plus syrups and flavoring extracts. Now,
puffing slightly, she was heading for liqueurs—Cointreau,
crème de cacao, and so forth. It's happily true that one can
acquire a variegated hoard of these things with less pain now
that the liqueur people are putting out so many of them in
half-pint sizes.

My friend also said she added something for texture if the
fruit didn't provide it and if she had it: chopped ginger, coconut, cookie crumbs, chocolate bits, crushed toffee. . . . I certainly wouldn't argue about a little thing like that.

The last five desserts in this chapter are hard to classify.
They're here mainly because they're dependable stand-bys in
a high wind—good, easy, and nearly foolproof. (I don't know
how you could go wrong on the Apple-Nut Pudding if you
remembered to shell the nuts.) Also, they're fancy or not, as
you like.

For example, this same Apple-Nut Pudding is homey as
great-grandma's kitchen if you serve it in an oatmeal bowl,
plain or with cream. But in a footed sherbet dish or a champagne glass, with softened vanilla ice cream spiked with rum,
it's quite all right for the carriage trade.

NEW HAMPSHIRE APPLE-NUT PUDDING

4-5 servings

(*Chewy, crisp, and fast*)
3 apples, unpeeled but chopped

½ cup walnuts or pecans
1 teaspoon baking powder
1 cup *sugar*
2 tablespoons *flour*
1 well-beaten egg

Mix the dry things together, but don't sift them. Add the apples and nuts, finally the egg, and put it all into a smallish baking dish. Bake at 350° for fifty minutes.

Similarly, the Immediate Fudge Cake, next, is plain or polite, depending on how it's served and with what.

IMMEDIATE FUDGE CAKE

(*As the name strongly suggests, this is rather fast. And you use only a saucepan for the mixing—no bowls. It's a firm-textured, rather chewy cake, and the pan is good to lick.*)

Melt ⅓ cup of butter in a saucepan, and into it squeeze two envelopes of the ready-blend unsweetened baking chocolate. (Or melt 2 squares of the regular kind, as you melt the butter.) Stir it, then add

1 cup sugar
2 eggs
½ teaspoon vanilla
¾ cup flour

¼ teaspoon salt
½ or ¾ cup coarsely chopped pecans or walnuts

Pour it into a greased brownie-type cake pan—that's about 8 inches square—and bake it at 375° for twenty-five minutes.

Just a word, by the way, or 101 words, to be accurate, about frostings.

In a sudden rush of inventiveness, some years ago, a home economist placed some chocolate-mint patties (or plain chocolate bars) on a hot fresh cake, reheated it two or three minutes, then spread them around. The idea spread like chocolate-mint patties (or chocolate bars) on a hot cake.

It is a good thing to know, although when the cake gets cold, the candy is going to revert to its original solid consistency. So it's best to eat the cake quickly. Good packaged or canned frosting is better. You could just dust this cake with powdered sugar, too. Or leave it alone.

Ditto for the next recipe, which is a great little recipe to know about, by the way. Bake it in a tube cake pan and pile slightly sweetened strawberries or peaches in the middle. Though you don't have to do that either, because it's jolly good anyway. It is called

THE CAKE

In a bowl, put

    1 package yellow cake mix (1 pound, 3 ounces)
    1 package instant vanilla pudding
    4 eggs (don't bother to beat them)
    ¾ cup salad oil
    ¾ cup sherry
    1 teaspoon nutmeg.

Now beat it all for 5 minutes, medium speed. Pour it into a greased tube cake pan or mold, and bake it 45 minutes at 350°.

Coming up now is a good modernized old-fashioned dessert that's a breeze with a blender or with canned puréed baby fruit. That is, I think it would work quite all right with canned baby fruit, though I haven't tried it, because there is a lot of work to writing a cookbook anyway. You have to try every idea that could turn out disastrous, which is nearly everything. And I don't see how this possibly could. Not top-hole, perhaps. But not disastrous.

A PUFFY PRUNE WHIP

    about 22 pitted cooked prunes (you can buy them in
        jars) or enough cooked dried apricots to make
        about a cup and a half of pulp. Or baby fruit
        likewise
    ½ cup orange marmalade
    1 tablespoon lemon juice
    ¾ cup broken walnut or pecan meats, for prunes;
        chopped toasted almonds, for apricots
    3 egg whites, beaten stiff with 2 tablespoons sugar

Put the prunes, marmalade, and lemon juice into the blender and blend till smooth—about six to eight seconds. Put it in a bowl, then fold in most of the nuts and the egg whites. Pile it into sherbet glasses and top with the rest of the nuts.

Finally, here is a wintertime hot canned-fruit dessert that's good and easy to organize. Mix it ahead, then put it in a 300°

oven to heat when you sit down. It needs only heating through.

It's best topped with commercial sour cream, whipped a bit with a fork. Don't use sweet cream you purposely soured with vinegar, which is an okay ingredient but a less-than-okay topping.

One other thing about this dessert: it's good as a side dish with an entree, served hot or cold. If you do serve it cold, heat it through once before you chill it.

HOT WINTER FRUIT

1 orange and 1 lemon	8-ounce can pineapple pieces
2 or 3 tablespoons light brown sugar	8-ounce can sliced peaches
8-ounce can apricots	8-ounce can pitted Bing cherries (or plums)

Grate the orange and lemon rinds into the brown sugar, then cut the orange and lemon pulps into thin slices, removing the seeds. Mix these slices with the rest of the fruit, and put a layer of it in a baking dish. Sprinkle it with part of the rind-and-sugar mix, and a spatter of nutmeg. Repeat the layers, then heat it in the 300° oven.

At the same time, place on top of the stove a ski boot or a pipe wrench or some other object that isn't customarily found there, if you can think of one. This may remind you, when you take the dish out, to *turn the oven off*.

Speaking as one who punctually turns off the oven every morning, before I fry the breakfast eggs, I know the importance of this, and the difficulty. The lads who designed our stoves believed they'd solved the problem when they thought up the signal light that's off when the oven is. But for preoccupied cooks, that's only a starter. We need an oven that trumpets and stomps like a mad bull elephant for ten minutes every night around 10:00 P.M.

Until they perfect one, keeping the oven on all night is just one of those luxuries that many of us don't especially enjoy but have to put up with.

"I sometimes despair of ever meeting my standards."
    —PETER DE VRIES

CHAPTER 10

Picnic, Going on a

WHAT EVER HAPPENED TO POTATO SALAD?

*"Some things are of that nature as to make
One's fancy chuckle, while his heart doth ache. . . ."*
—JOHN BUNYAN

Ever since someone discovered that it is possible to make a picnic as complicated as a six-course dinner, the picnic picture has been cloudy as the probable weather on picnic day.

You used to know where you stood or sat at a picnic, besides right in the poison oak, because picnics used to come in four standard stanzas, like "The Star-Spangled Banner":

the fried chicken
the potato salad
the stuffed eggs and relishes
the cake and the fruit.

But now the whole thing seems to have been upgraded while many of us weren't looking. The fire you see in yonder dell isn't for toasting marshmallows; it's the Cherries Jubilee, flaming nicely. You're apt to find almost anything on picnics these days, from Sole Amandine to Dutch Curry, if you can believe what you read in the public prints, and sometimes you can.

Well, then, it might logically be asked: "If the picnic has escalated on us like this, why bother with it?"

The answer is twofold.

For one thing, giving a picnic is still easier than giving a dinner party, because it bypasses several big problems: house cleaning, table setting, timing. Remember this is a *picnic* we're talking about, out of reach of the house, not a backyard barbecue or a patio party, either of which usually means about as much work as you'd have done otherwise, including hot-and-cold-running canapés, with you doing most of the running. The legwork for the hostess at these things can be tremendous.

Also, your guests are quite as indebted to you, if you did the whole picnic, as though you'd entertained them at home. We'll presently come to a couple of points worth observing if this is a hearty group endeavor, with you as the organizer.

Therefore, let's spread out the blanket in this nice little patch of clover and take a look at the view, which includes some picnics and some picnic situations in which you might find yourself.

There are several ways to upgrade your own picnics, if you think it's indicated. Depending on the folkways of the group, one way is to start thinking in terms of wine instead of beer. And to bring wineglasses. Wine in a paper cup is a shame (although, as in Picnic 4, it's better than none).

Too, it's good to keep in mind the words of M. Raymond Oliver, official ambassador of the cuisine Française, and owner of the historic Paris restaurant Le Grand Vefour. In San Francisco recently, after ordering a seafood salad for lunch, he said, "Bring us a red California wine, a Cabernet Sauvignon, and be sure to chill it."

And, he continued, to the party at large, "I don't see why we should let our tastes be dictated by some code. I like red wine, even with fish, and prefer it chilled. Who is going to tell me what I must or must not drink with such a dish?"

So let's not fret about these things. Run your own ship.

The next step in upgrading your picnic is to upgrade the Standard Picnic Menu we just passed. So let's do that.

1. *The upgraded chicknic*

If you can buy good whole rotisseried or otherwise barbecued chickens where you live, do so, allowing one for two people—split, so that each gets half.

If you can't, make Bastard Barbecue, on page 45, which is a swift, satisfactory way to cook a lot of chicken. Allow two or three pieces per customer.

The upgraded salad could be

NON-POTATO SALAD

6 servings

(This turns out to be a bulgur salad, with considerable class. Some other time you could add fresh crab, lobster, or shrimp, and serve it as an entree.)

Pour 2 cups of boiling water over 1 cup of bulgur wheat. Let it stand about two hours, or till the wheat has absorbed the water.

Add

> ¼ cup garlic wine vinegar
> ¼ cup olive oil

and chill it. Then add

> 1 small jar sliced green stuffed olives
> ½ cup chopped green onions and stems
> ½ cup chopped parsley
> 2 or 3 chopped tomatoes
> 2 cups finely chopped raw spinach
> salt, pepper, celery salt

Put it all in a salad bowl, and lay some green peppers and onion rings on top. Chill.

As a dressing, bring along in a separate jar mayonnaise mixed with a little curry and vinegar.

Bread could be breadsticks.

You'll need no stuffed eggs and relishes. They'd taste a little repetitious.

For the upgraded dessert, fresh fruit is good, anything but bananas.[1]

---

[1] Raw bananas haven't made it socially. I think that's because they don't begin with a p. But take pears, now, or pineapple or peaches or papayas or plums. . . . Prunes are a moot fruit, of course, except in situations like the fruit whip on page 129.

Or you could bring a frozen cheesecake from the luxury-frozen-foods department. Or a frozen German Chocolate Cake, ditto. Or a rich fruitcake, which, being unexpected, has more appeal at picnic time than at Christmas time.

Another version of the upgraded picnic is

2. *The champagne turknic*

Take a boned rolled turkey out of its can, wrap it in foil or plastic wrap, and bring it, along with a sharp knife. (Or pack one of the frozen turkey arrangements, all white or white-and-dark meat that you cook in its own pan. In that case, cook it first.)

Bring, as well, some chilled domestic champagne in a tub of ice, one bottle per four people. If you look around, you can find it remarkably low-priced, and it adds fizz to the occasion.

Also, bring a loaf each of good brown bread and good white bread, the type small bakeries pride themselves on, plus some butter, mayonnaise, salt, and pepper. People may want to make their own sandwiches. Even if they don't, you needn't. As the madam of the picnic, you have other things on your mind, and they can eat their turkey sliced.

Bring a salad bowl, too, with salad greenery in a plastic bag. (Have it crisp, torn, and ready when you put it into the plastic bag, then put the bag in an ice chest or a dishpan with ice in it.) Bring croutons (page 98) and a jar of Ready Caesar Salad Dressing (page 98).

For relish, the classic uncooked cranberry-and-orange is good, and certainly easy. The day before the picnic, grind together, in the blender or otherwise, 1 quart of raw cranberries and 1 whole orange (chunked first, if you use the blender). Mix in 2 cups of sugar and store it in covered jars in the refrigerator till picnic time.

With the bread, plus the croutons in the salad, you needn't bother with rolls or potatoes.

A painless dessert here would be a big box of chocolates, to keep passing around.

The final upgraded picnic is

3. *The roasted sirloin tipnic*

Roast the meat slightly pinker than you ordinarily would.

Bring along a peanut-butter jar of sour-cream-and-horse-radish dressing. (Add horseradish and lemon juice to sour cream, tasting as you go.)

Bring a cooked artichoke per person, and mayonnaise.

Bring a loaf of prebuttered French bread.

If men are involved in this picnic, as they so often are, you might want something heavy. For instance:

FAR-OUT POTATO SALAD

6 servings

Cook, peel, and drain 5 good-sized potatoes, then slice them into a bowl. Pour a half-cup of sauterne over them, and leave them alone for a couple of hours, till the potatoes drink the wine. While they're living it up, mix together

⅓ cup Wishbone Italian Dressing
4 green onions, chopped
⅔ cup sliced cauliflowerets
2 coarsely chopped pimentos
½ teaspoon salt
1 tablespoon bottled capers, drained.[2]

Put this in the refrigerator, in a covered jar.

Bring the bowl of spuds and the dressing separately to the picnic, and mix the two thoroughly just before you serve it. Parsley on top is nice but not vital.

A big thing about picnics, by the way, is to make sure there are plenty of napkins.

Not long ago I was invited to a picnic that proved educational. When we'd finished eating, the hostess handed around small, steamy-hot scented towels, as they do on the daintier airlines. It was an impressive piece of business, I can tell you, and refreshing, too.

[2] You don't usually have capers around, and they seem expensive. But a jarful lasts and lasts—mine's on its second year now—and they add a festive little kick in the pants to certain fish things and salads.

I asked her how she did it. She said she adds a good dash of her husband's cologne (the poor fellow always gets some for Christmas) to hot water. Then, wearing lined rubber gloves, she wrings them out and drops them into a preheated wide-mouthed gallon Thermos jug.

I wouldn't go to that trouble myself, but I like to go to her picnics.

Another good thing to remember to bring is several big brown paper sacks, which are so handy at cleaning-up time.

Next, we come to a picnic that's tailor-made for the unwilling cook. I refer to the

4. *A and p-icnic*

This type can simply happen, or—with a little forethought and artistry—you can make it happen. It fits nicely into an en route situation on a beautiful day, when restaurants seem stuffy. Properly promoted, it goes down well with people who have happy memories of *la pique-nique* in France or roadside lunches outside Lisbon.

In the car's glove compartment, keep salt, pepper, and a knife, just in case. Then, when you come to a likely looking grocery or market, pick up

> salami[3]
> pumpernickel or French bread
> cheese
> butter
> whatever fresh fruit looks good
> a bottle of wine and some paper cups.

For plates you may use the paper the food came wrapped in, and the knife can be enjoyed by all.

Finally, we come to the Potluck (or Everyone-Bring-Something) Picnic, which is popular in many circles. But it has caused unnecessary misery through lack of planning. As the third bowl of the same thing turns up, you begin to think

---

[3] Or liver sausage. Or Polish sausage . . . Not Bologna, though, or the strange jellied affairs you sometimes see. One slice of jellied Cheddar-and-veal loaf and you've lost your Continental accent.

you're celebrating National Eat-More-Baked-Beans Week, or Macaroni, as the case may be.

Definitely, the Potluck Picnic should be masterminded by someone. If you find you're It, as a result of an off-guard moment, you could do it this way:

You state that you're bringing the entree—say, Bastard Barbecue—and the wine. You'll also be responsible for

plates	napkins
cups	ice
glasses	salt and pepper.
cutlery	

Announce with equal clarity that Couple #2 will bring

baked beans or a	bread or rolls, and butter
hearty salad (her choice)	relishes

and Couple #3 will bring

fresh fruit	coffee
cheese	cake or cookies.

If someone is left over, he might be gifted with janitorial details: going back to the car for the ice and the gnat-bite lotion, unloading, and, finally, loading up again. I've always believed that Maud Muller on a summer's day raking the meadows sweet with hay was hunting for the salt shaker.

On the other hand, if you're an organizee rather than the organizer, you will probably find your own morale holds up better when you bring something a bit different, even though it's not necessarily better: Gorgonzola instead of Swiss cheese, Japanese persimmons instead of peaches, spiced kumquats instead of pickles. Something, that is, with a modicum of flair.

Not that everyone has to.

Once upon a summertime I went to a potluck picnic (I brought that Non-Potato Salad) to which a gourmet cook of considerable local standing was invited, too. Her assignment had been dessert. So, at dessert time, she brought out big cellophane sacks of old-fashioned grocery-store plump choc-olate-marshmallow cookies.

"I adore these, don't you?" she beamed, handing them around. And everyone did, thinking, moreover, *How original, how posh!* But if someone else had done this, they'd have thought, *Poor child, how naïve!*

Mrs. Tiffany can wear ten-cent beads, and J. Paul Getty can wear out-at-the-elbow sweaters, too. That's the way the world runs, and no one has figured out yet what to do about it.

CHAPTER 11

Specialty, The Regional or Foreign

I GUESS YOU ALWAYS LOSE A LITTLE IN THE TRANSLATION

"Animals will expend energy to introduce variability into an otherwise constant or consistent situation even when there is no extrinsic reward."
—BERNARD BERELSON and GARY A. STEINER

As we just saw in the previous chapter, an element of cookmanship occasionally confuses the kitchen picture, the way béarnaise complicates a steak. And it isn't easy to make any sort of showing, especially if you don't want to very much or very often.

However, when you do, it's likely that you'll have the best luck with the Regional or Foreign Specialty, though even here it isn't plain sailing. Indeed, the specialty poses an interesting problem, alive with pros and cons. Let's consider first its disadvantages.

For one, any dish tends to lose some of its charm when you get it home, away from the sound of the temple bells or the cable cars (just as a pretty little wet rock you find at the beach isn't quite so pretty dry on your kitchen window sill). When you've gone to the trouble of making it, only to find those important intangibles missing, something within you dies.

Nor is it roses all the way for the guest. If you're serving your *pissaladière* after the manner of the Niçoise to people who haven't been where you've been, all they will taste is the *pissaladière*. If they are treated, into the bargain, to a full description of that off-the-beaten-track restaurant where you discovered it—that tiny, picturesque place where they spoke only Diners' Club—they are going to feel that the evening is longer than it actually is.

In addition, some regional or foreign specialties are better than others, depending on the region. Indeed, you would suspect certain recipes from certain regions of having been ridden out of there, on a rail. I'd like to have seen the Scotch haggis leaving town.

On the other hand, some are good and also surprisingly easy to make. For instance, I used to regard with simple awe those people who had the temerity to make Scotch Shortbread. Then I found that it's slightly simpler than a peanut-butter sandwich.

This holds true for a number of well-known dishes. If you can't make Alfredo's Fettuccine, for another example, you're in real trouble. And such a plus factor mustn't be minimized by the reluctant cook.

Therefore, given this advantage, a slight Otherwhere aura can be another. Maui Banana Bread, for example, spreads some *aloha* around, while Mrs. Womack's Banana Bread does not, although the recipes happen to be identical. (Mr. and Mrs. Womack once visited Hawaii and had a very nice time, too.) Similarly, a Croque Monsieur has it all over a grilled cheese sandwich.

One important thing: if you are going to specialize in a regional specialty, it is wise to choose one from a region other than your own. That is, if you live in Oregon, near the Columbia River, it's better to specialize in Kentucky Corn Pone than in Columbia River Salmon, for those tireless Oregon cooks have worked that stream pretty thoroughly and developed numerous refinements. One lady adds a spatter of

Chablis, another counters with herbed sour cream. . . . So it goes, and you're not up to that kind of infighting.

As a general rule, then, the farther away your specialty came from, the better.[1] And in this fast-frozen jet age, ingredients for most things are generally available, at least for our modest purposes here.

And so to an Alphabet of regional or foreign dishes that taste quite all right and are easy to make—no pitfalls or pratfalls or sudden sauces.

Some are classics, although here and there a few nonessentials have been omitted (the same way editors cut chunks out of Sir Walter Scott without hurting him much).

ANTIPASTO

A first course of antipasto is easy and attractive, as well as helpful if you don't think the roast will quite stretch. You can serve it in the living room, too, passing out individual plates and forks, then the platter. This will alert the guests that they're on the last drink.

On a large platter, arrange several or all of these:

> curried deviled eggs
> thin-sliced Italian salami or Italian or Polish ham from the delicatessen
> crescents of cantaloupe or honeydew
> best-grade sardines
> black olives
> artichoke hearts, vinaigretted (These come in jars. Or you can cook frozen ones and marinate them in vinegar-and-oil dressing.)
> cherry tomatoes
> radishes
> white albacore tuna (sprinkled with lemon juice and pepper)
> mild Italian peppers

---

[1] Should someone indicate an uncalled-for familiarity with the dish anyway, you can say casually, "This is rather an interesting version of Chlodnik, don't you think?" which implies that you're familiar with other versions.

BOILED-BEEF VIENNESE

4-5 servings

Boiled beef sounds flat as a matzo, which is too bad, because it's quite good, especially with horseradish. So perhaps you'd better call it Tafelspitz.

    2 pounds beef chuck and 2 or 3 beef bones
    1 teaspoon salt
    3 peppercorns
    a carrot and a celery stalk and 2 small onions
    handful of parsley tied in a cheesecloth bag

Put everything in a kettle or Dutch oven with water to cover. After it comes to a boil, lower it to simmer, and simmer it covered about three hours (or till the beef is tender). STOP HERE. Then reheat it, slice the beef, and eat it, with plain horseradish, or with horseradish mixed to taste with whipped cream and lemon juice.

(If you cool and skim the fat, then strain the broth and season it with some pepper, salt, and nutmeg, it's a good soup for another time.)

CROQUE MONSIEUR

Croquer means "to munch," so this would seem to be a simple directive.

    16 slices good bread (not the squeezable kind)
    16 slices of Gruyère or Swiss cheese
    8 slices ham, boiled or baked, just so it's good
    butter

Actually, this is a sandwich within a sandwich. Put a slice of ham between 2 slices of cheese, then a slice of buttered bread on either side. Fry it gently in butter. (You could French-toast it instead and they won't take away your chef's apron. First dip it in egg and milk beaten together, *then* fry it in butter.)

DANISH ALMOND SHEET

makes 2-2½ dozen

Rich easy cookies you bake in one big piece.

½ pound butter   2 beaten eggs

1 cup sugar

¼ pound chopped almonds

4¼ cups flour

granulated sugar

(to sprinkle on top)

Melt the butter, then add everything else except the topping sugar, mix it, and cool it a bit.

Now put it in the middle of a cookie sheet and press it out gently but fervently, in the hope that it will cover the whole thing. It may, then again it may not. In any case, sprinkle it with sugar, and bake it for about twelve minutes at 375° till it's golden-brown. Cut it in squares, rectangles, or rhomboids.

EDDY'S OYSTER LOAVES

6 *servings*

Eddy was a San Franciscan who owned a bar and made small oyster loaves for his married male customers to take home to their wives. These were pacifiers. But Eddy is dead now, and Mother must pacify herself.

This is good for a special lunch. I also know a family who has it traditionally as Christmas Eve supper.

    3 dozen fresh oysters
    3 small loaves French bread
    ½ teaspoon garlic powder
    4 tablespoons melted butter
    milk

First, almost split the loaves lengthwise, leaving a hinge. Scoop out the soft middles and save the crumbs. Then add a half-teaspoonful of garlic powder (not salt) to 2 tablespoons of melted butter, and crush the cavities.

Next, drain the oysters and save the liquor. Sauté them in the other 2 tablespoons of butter till the edges curl—about five minutes.

Put the oysters into the loaves, mix the crumbs you saved with the oyster liquor you saved, and add them, too. Shut up the loaves now. STOP HERE.

Then wrap them in cheesecloth dipped in milk, twisting the ends and tucking them under the loaf. Bake them on a baking sheet for half an hour at 350°. Cut them in half before you serve them.

FETTUCCINE ALFREDO

Two things are important here: 1) to use Parmesan cheese

you grated yourself,[2] and 2) to toss the noodles vigorously, with controlled abandon, so that each and every millimeter of every one is covered with the butter and cheese.

4 servings

    8 ounces broad egg noodles
    ½ pound butter
    ½ pound Parmesan

Cook the noodles till they're tender—about ten minutes. Drain them well. Put them in a hot bowl, add butter cut in chunks (melted butter would give it a non-Alfredo flavor) and add the grated cheese. Then mix.

GREEN GODDESS SALAD DRESSING

This is the well-known San Francisco salad dressing named from the old George Arliss play. There are dozens of variations of it, including bottled. I like this one the best of those I've tasted. In these proportions it dresses 10 servings, and if you're not serving 10, so much the better. It keeps well, and you use the rest as a dressing for broccoli or asparagus. It's also a good dip for artichoke leaves.

(As to what you put the dressing on—classically speaking —it's greenery: any lettuce or watercress or whatever you have, with tomato wedges on top. If it's to be the main course, add crabmeat, shrimps, or chunks of cold chicken along with the tomatoes.)

Mix 1 tablespoon lemon juice with ½ cup whipping cream. Then add and mix

1 cup mayonnaise[3]
3 tablespoons tarragon vinegar
3 tablespoons regular cider vinegar
1 crushed garlic clove
1 rounded tablespoon anchovy paste
⅓ cup fresh parsley
2 tablespoons onion powder (or 1 tablespoon instant minced onion).

[2] This is what the purists say. I have not been able to discern much difference, myself, and I've tried. However, the kind you grate yourself you *know* is freshly grated, and you don't know how long ago the grocer's was.

[3] The recipe actually calls for "good mayonnaise," a term that alway makes me feel truculent as well as defensive. What kind do they think you buy? I'm sure whatever you have is all right, so long as it isn't Salad Dressing.

HOMINY, SOUTHERN STYLE

serves 6 people who will eat hominy

Some people like hominy. Some, who ordinarily don't, may like it this way. Maybe the butter and slow baking do something. At any rate, you can bake it right along with a roast.

¾ cup hominy grits	1 egg slightly beaten
1 teaspoon salt	2 cups milk
¼ cup butter	1 cup water
1 teaspoon sugar	

Mix the hominy grits with the water and salt, and stir it to get rid of the lumps. Boil it for two minutes.

Then add a cup of milk and simmer it an hour, with an occasional stir. Finally, add the butter, sugar, egg, the rest of the milk, put it in a buttered casserole, and STOP HERE. Eventually, bake it, uncovered, for an hour at 325°.

IRISH SODA BREAD

This is a big easy crusty faintly sweet biscuit (you cut it in wedges), comforting as a turf fire in a thatched cottage. It is handy when you're out of bread.

2 cups flour	½ cup raisins or currants
½ teaspoon soda	¾ cup sour milk (add a
1½ teaspoon baking powder	tablespoon of vinegar to
½ teaspoon salt	sweet milk and let it set
1 tablespoon sugar	five minutes)
4 tablespoons shortening	1 tablespoon caraway seeds

Operate as you do for biscuits: sift the dry ingredients, cut in the shortening, add the raisins and caraway seeds. Add the milk, knead it all a moment, shape it into a round loaf about ¾-inch thick, and put it in a greased pan. Bake thirty minutes at 375°.

JACOBBERGER RAVIOLI

6-8 servings

One trouble with an Alphabet is that it usually lets you down at least once before you even get to X. This is what happened with J. It was a choice between a complicated Jambalaya and a nonessential Jelly Roll, and so I chose Ravioli, and named it for Jean Jacobberger, herself.

The basic procedure here is: 1) you make a sauce, 2) you make a filling, and 3) you layer them with cooked macaroni.

As you can see, it isn't a classic ravioli at all, but it's a ring-tailed snorter as an entree or a side dish for a buffet.

The sauce

Brown 1½ pounds of ground beef in 2 tablespoons of olive oil. Then add, and simmer twenty minutes

> 1 can tomato sauce
> 1 small can tomatoes
> ½ cup water
> 1 package French's Spaghetti Sauce mix.

The macaroni

Cook ½ pound of bowknot-shaped macaroni till nearly done, then drain it.

The filling

Mix together

medium can spinach, drained and chopped	½ cup grated Parmesan
½ cup parsley, chopped	1 clove garlic, minced
½ cup fine dry bread crumbs	2 tablespoons olive oil
Sit down a minute.	3 beaten eggs.

Then layer these three items in a flat baking dish—sauce, macaroni, filling, sauce, macaroni, filling. Cover it with Parmesan. STOP HERE. Bake it, uncovered, for thirty minutes at 350°.

KANSAS CITY BEEFBURGERS

In Kansas City, when they grow weary of hamburgers plain, they sometimes spoon this sauce over the hot meat.

Blend or otherwise mix thoroughly

> ½ pound blue cheese
> ½ cup softened margarine or butter
> ¼ teaspoon garlic powder
> 2 tablespoons prepared mustard
> salt and pepper as you like it.

LOUISVILLE LOBSTER (OR CRABMEAT)

8 servings

This should be served with a Southern accent and a camellia. It's rich and fairly expensive. But it is a good special supper with only a salad and rolls, and it can be fixed completely ahead.

¼ cup butter
¼ teaspoon garlic powder
chopped parsley
1 No. 2½ can tomatoes
    (or 3½ cups)
¼ cup flour
½ cup cream

2 tablespoons Worcestershire
    sauce
½ cup sherry
4 cups cooked lobster or
    crabmeat
2 cans browned-in-butter
    mushrooms

Put the garlic powder in half the butter in a saucepan and simmer it a minute. Then add the chopped parsley and 3 cups of the tomatoes.

While it cooks, mix the flour with the other half-cup of tomatoes till it's a smooth paste, then add it to the first to-mato mixture. Cook it just a minute, then mix in the cream, Worcestershire, and sherry. Cook *that* five minutes, mix in the seafood and mushrooms, salt and pepper it, and pour it into a casserole dish. Sprinkle it with any sort of crumbs you have, dot it with the butter that's left, and STOP HERE. Bake it, uncovered, for twenty minutes at 375°.

MAUI BANANA BREAD

I think a Maui mama invented this when she let some bananas get a bit too ripe to eat. It's good toasted for Sunday breakfast, too. You can *luau* yourself a slice of ham to go with it.

2 cups sugar
1 cup shortening
6 ripe bananas, mashed
4 eggs, well beaten

2½ cups cake flour
1 teaspoon salt
2 teaspoons baking powder

Cream the sugar and shortening, then add the mashed bananas and eggs. Sift the dry ingredients and add them, but don't overmix it. Bake it in a greased loaf pan at 350° for about thirty-five minutes. (Give it the broomstraw test in the middle.)

NORTHWESTERN CRAB AND WILD RICE

This comes from the wilds of Portland, Oregon, where they have good crabmeat. The more mushrooms, the more people it will serve. As is, it serves 8, if you're also providing a fair-sized green or fresh-fruit salad, for instance, and rolls.

½ pound wild rice
1½ pounds crabmeat
1 can condensed mushroom soup
½ cup light cream

    1 cup grated cheese (Swiss or Cheddar)
    mushrooms, if you like—a couple cans of the
       browned-in-butter kind or ¼ pound of fresh
       mushrooms sautéed in 2 tablespoons of butter

Cook the rice as the package says to.

Dilute the soup with the cream. Then, in a casserole dish, layer it—rice, crabmeat, soup (with mushrooms added, if any) and cheese. Keep right on till it's full. STOP HERE. Bake it, covered, for thirty minutes at 350°. Uncover it at the last if the cheese hasn't melted.

O'FLANAGAN'S SAUSAGE SUPPER

4-5 servings

Good and hearty for a cold night, and, with instant mashed potatoes, not much work.

    1 pound pork sausage, link or bulk (if it's bulk, shape
       it into cakes)
    2 apples, pared and sliced
    2 onions, peeled and sliced
    1 tablespoon flour
    salt and pepper
    1 cup bouillon (cube or powder kind)
    2 or 3 cups hot instant mashed potatoes

Fry the sausage till it's crisp. Drain it, then put it in a baking dish. In the fat that's left, cook the apples and onions until they're tender, then spoon them over the sausage.

Pour off all but a tablespoon of the fat now, and brown the flour in it. Add the salt, pepper, and bouillon, stir till it's a bit thicker, and pour it over the sausage and so forth. Top it with the mashed potatoes. STOP HERE. Bake for fifteen minutes, uncovered, at 350°.

PICAYUNE PECAN PIE
(OR, JUST A DAB FOR ME)

This pie is astonishingly fast and easy. The hard part is parting with the price of the nuts. However, owing to its richness, one pie serves 8 to 10 people, or the same two or three several times, for it keeps well.

A good way to serve it is to arrange small wedges on a

plate and punctuate them with small clusters of cold white grapes.

You need an unbaked pie shell.

You also need

3 eggs	1 tablespoon sherry
½ cup heavy cream less 1 tablespoon	½ cup dark corn syrup
	⅛ teaspoon salt
1 cup sugar	1½ cups pecans, plus enough
1 teaspoon vanilla	to ornament the top.
2 tablespoons butter	

Put everything into the blender in that order, except for those decorative pecan halves. Turn the blender on for about ten seconds (just count "1 pecan, 2 pecans, 3 pecans . . ." if yours is a quaint old early-American blender without a timer, like mine).

Pour it in the pie shell and bake it at 400° for twenty-five minutes, then decorate it with the pecan halves and bake for ten minutes more. (If the middle seems shaky then, it might take another five.) Cool it before serving.

QUICHE LORRAINE À LA SUISSE

6 servings

This isn't the classic *quiche,* because it contains Swiss cheese.

Line a pie pan with pastry.

Fill it about half full with alternating layers of chopped boiled ham (or crisp bacon bits) and diced Swiss cheese, starting with the cheese. You'll need about half a pound of each.

STOP HERE.

Then beat together

> 5 eggs
> 1 cup of light cream
> ½ teaspoon salt.

Pour it over the cheese and ham, then bake it at 350° for forty-five minutes. Serve it in wedges.

REALLY SOUTHERN CORN BREAD

6 servings

This is from Texas via Oklahoma, and sugarless—which classicists insist on—and fast.

Beat together with a fork an egg and a teaspoon of salt.

Then add, beating slightly with the same fork between additions

> 1 cup milk
> 2 heaping teaspoons baking powder
> ⅓ cup flour
> 1¼ cups white or yellow corn meal.

In a middle-sized skillet melt 2 level tablespoons of shortening. Pour most of it into the batter, leaving just a little. Pour the batter into the skillet, put the skillet in the oven, and bake it for twenty-five minutes at 425°. Cut it like a pie and serve it hot.

SCOTCH SHORTBREAD

For Scotsmen in a hurry. Good, too.

> ½ pound butter
> 3 cups flour
> ¼ cup sugar

Cream the butter and sugar, then add the flour. It will be stiff and rather crumbly but forge ahead, pressing it into a square 8-inch pan. Bake it at 300° for an hour. Cool it ten minutes, then cut it in squares.

TOMATOES PROVENCAL

6 servings

This seems to make a tomato go farther than it normally would.

First you scoop the seeds and some of the pulp out of six big tomatoes cut in half. Salt and pepper them, then turn them upside down somewhere so they'll drain.

Mix up

a minced garlic clove	¾ teaspoon dried basil
2 tablespoons chopped green onions	¼ teaspoon thyme
	¾ cup bread crumbs

with enough olive oil to hold it together and help stuff it in the tomatoes. STOP HERE. Then sprinkle a bit more oil on top and bake them, uncovered, for fifteen minutes at 400°.

URUGUAY OMELET

6 servings

This omelet never saw Uruguay, but the woman who gave me the recipe did. She said it tasted like lunch there.

> 1 7-ounce can of green chili sauce (Ortega Green Chile Salsa is a good brand)

6 eggs
3 tablespoons milk
¼ teaspoon salt
3 tablespoons butter
¾ cup grated cheese

Have the chili sauce heating in a little pan while you beat the eggs, milk, and salt. Melt the butter in a skillet or omelet pan, then pour in the egg mixture and cook till it's nearly firm. Cover half the omelet with half the sauce and half the cheese. Fold it, then pour the rest on top.

VEAL SCALLOPINI

3-4 servings

This is a good nonsweet scallopini, which is rather hard to find.

1 pound veal round steak, well trimmed
½ cup grated Parmesan
salt and pepper

Pound the cheese into both sides of the meat with a blunt instrument. Keep pounding till the cheese is used up and the meat is a scant ¼-inch thick. Salt and pepper both sides, cut the meat in 2-inch strips, then sauté them in olive oil.

Now add

a crushed garlic clove
½ cup beef broth
2 tablespoons lemon juice

½ teaspoon marjoram
¼ teaspoon thyme
½ cup dry white wine.

Cover it. STOP HERE. Then simmer for half an hour. If you like, you can add some sautéed mushrooms or sliced stuffed green olives, but you don't have to.

WESTERN SANDWICH

2 large servings

This is called Western in the East and Denver in the West. The other day I ran across a variation of it called an East-Western Sandwich, which was probably invented by a Chinese cowboy. It called for water chestnuts and soy sauce, but didn't taste as good as the classic version, which follows. It's too good a sandwich to forget, and the ingredients are usually around.

4 eggs
¼ green pepper, chopped

2 teaspoons chopped onion
salt and pepper

Melt 2 tablespoons of butter in a skillet. Sauté the green pepper and onion in it for a few minutes. Pour in the eggs, add the salt and pepper, and cook it till it's firm. Serve on buttered toast, open face.

ZABAGLIONE
(OR, PLEASE, NOT WHILE WE'RE EATING)

I made zabaglione once for four people and it turned out nicely. Dizzy with success then, I decided to make it for ten people. But one absent-minded moment with zabaglione and you have Chinese Egg Soup, which is what I got.

Thus can Providence punish those who try to show off with zabaglione. It's best to try to show off with something else.

So, on second thought, I won't include the recipe, lest it get someone else into trouble.

CHAPTER 12

Tail Gate, Shutting the

NOW WHAT DID I FORGET THIS TIME?

"Farther along we'll know all about it . . .
Farther along we'll understand why. . . ."
—GOSPEL SONG

Like a love affair, a cookbook is probably easier to get into than out of. At the end of both, sins of commission and omission loom large. What was said that had better been left unsaid? Is the chocolate sauce really that good?[1] And what was not said that might have been? Shouldn't there have been some mention of brunches?[2]

In writing a cookbook, it is the possible omissions that are

[1] Yes.
[2] No.

especially worrisome. The trouble is, a paragraph or a chapter can unexpectedly close its doors, leaving a perfectly good item outside. There stands the Mustard Sauce, looking for the ham. Or a shapely hypothesis with no place to sit down.

That Mustard Sauce, by the way, runs into other things, as so many sauces do. Therefore we may as well get into it now, in the hope that the impetus will drive us a little farther around the track, at least to the clubhouse turn.

Here is the situation: many a devout noncook depends heavily on a canned cooked ham for emergencies, like those times when she doesn't feel like cooking. This ham stays in the refrigerator, diminishing steadily once it is opened (for these emergency periods can last several days). But it doesn't quite disappear, because it's replaced by another, just before the shortage becomes critical. This is known as the ham-in-residence.

Now the ham-in-residence is perfectly good as is, which is the reason it is there. But on the third or fourth day, a simple sauce can provide a nice change of pace. This one has the additional advantage of tasting good on the neighboring vegetables, if they happen to be broccoli, or asparagus, or Brussels sprouts, or string beans.

GOLD SAUCE

In the top of a double boiler mix ½ cup of sugar with 4 teaspoons of dry mustard and 1 teaspoon of salt.

In a bowl beat 2 eggs in ½ cup of milk, pour this into the dry mixture, then add ½ cup of vinegar and ¼ cup of melted butter.

Cook it over gently boiling water for fifteen minutes.

Now, something fast to go *with* the ham, if you're out of potato chips and time, is

MOTHER BRADFORD'S RICE

6-8 servings

*(Since Mother Bradford discovered this one,
her family hasn't tasted a baked potato.)*

In a saucepan put

1 can Campbell's onion soup
1 cup of rice, any kind
1 cup of water.

Cook it covered over medium heat until the rice is tender —about 25 minutes.

Another good thing to do with the h-in-r is the informal

EGGS BENEDICT

Toast an English muffin half, butter it, lay a slice of warm ham on it, and a poached egg on top of that. Cover it with the Huntley-Brinkley Hollandaise on page 116. Asparagus goes very nicely with this.

Then, one other ploy I know of will sometimes distract attention from Ham Again. It's nearly as easy as Bisquick Biscuits, which is mainly what it is, but it is livelier.

FAST CHEESE BREAD

Mix together

> 2 cups biscuit mix
> ½ cup grated Cheddar
> 2 tablespoons instant minced onion.

Add a beaten egg to it now, and ½ cup of milk plus 2 tablespoons. Stir till it's just moistened, then spread it out in a greased cake pan, and on the top sprinkle another ½ cup of cheese and a lot of poppy seeds. Bake it for twenty minutes or so at 400°, till it's a lovely brown, like a freckled palomino.

So much for the ham then. It's a relief to get it cleaned up.

Right here, while we're still at the table, might be the place for a minor point that wouldn't fit in anywhere else, and it has been troubling me. I refer to the occasional value of television at the family meal.

It isn't all bad, though a delicate snobbery prevails in some groups that hold that televiewing at the table ranks with putting the catsup bottle on it. Still many people do that, too.[3]

The fact is, the family's evening meal isn't always the lightsome, stimulating occasion it is in the picture books, with Dick and Jane happily describing their school field trip through the glass factory, and Mother and Father acting

[3]They probably wouldn't if the catsup people would pack it in squat wide-mouthed pots, so it could be served in something pretty and then replaced. But nearly everyone has better things to do with her time than trying to reinsert catsup into a catsup bottle.

motherly and fatherly. Families are sometimes cross, as a result of too much togetherness—possibly a hangover from a long day *en famille* in the car, or a rainy session at the beach, or the sniffles, or simply the daily stresses that come from living around the clock.

Many fathers seem to feel put upon 32% of their dinner-times. And mothers feel especially so when Dick and Jane snoot the food she thinks they ought to eat, and which she reluctantly but dutifully cooked.

At such times, perhaps she should keep in mind some words of Dr. William Kalb, consultant to the U.S. Food and Drug Administration. "Unless a child is sick, he should eat just as much as he wants to," Dr. Kalb said, in 1966. He continued: "There's no reason for a child to eat a particular food unless he wants to. If he doesn't want fish when he's six, he may want it when he's 16—if you don't force the issue. There is no one food such as fish or spinach that is vital. If a child doesn't get his nutrients one way, he can get them another."

And, summing it up, he says, "Let the child eat what he wants, providing he has enough protein, vitamins, and carbo-hydrates. For instance, if he wants spaghetti and hamburgers every day of the year, as long as he has some fruit too, it's okay."

This could be of some small comfort. But I'm afraid I dis-agree with Dr. Kalb's assertion that there's no reason for a child to eat a particular food unless he wants to. No one should grow up with a totally unadventurous palate, or he'll miss out on a lot of fun. Too, some tastes are acquired, and he might as well start acquiring them, the sooner the better, for everyone. Moreover, he should learn that an untouched plateful can hurt people's feelings, even his mother's.

However, when the atmosphere becomes sticky, for these and other possible reasons, a good television news program can keep everyone from brooding over how unpleasant every-one else is.

The children will learn more from it than they do from their father's "Butter, please." And the lady who cooked the dinner can get her mind off the whole thing and onto South-east Asia or Off Broadway, or wherever the action is. (If ptelevision ptomaine seems imminent as a result of the com-mercials, she can switch to a home-produced record program, with possibly more beneficial results.)

One more note belongs here—a few words for the family, not the cook.

As good audiences make good theater, good eaters make good—and happier—cooks. Though the reluctant cook will never really enjoy her kitchen work, punctuality, kind words, and clean plates are the carrots that will keep the little donkey plugging along.

Moreover, her family is in the perilous position of the trash-hauling company's clientele who received the notice: "Satisfaction guaranteed or twice your garbage back." Bouquets get better results than spitballs; and families had best keep this in mind if for no other reason than survival.

But space runs out, and we're on page 156 now, with things still left over, like the unwashed skillet you usually find the minute you've cleaned the sink.

I had hoped to be able to mention the semi-recipe which a gentlewoman of my acquaintance says has saved her hide at many a lunch and supper time. She heats a can of tuna mixed with a can of undiluted condensed cream of mushroom soup, then fills avocado halves with it, covers them with crumbs, and bakes them for twenty minutes at 350°.

Then, somehow or other, the sesame seeds got lost. I wanted to explain that if you toast one side of bread under the broiler, then butter the other, spread it thickly with sesame seeds, and brown *that* under the broiler, it's good for breakfast. And, cut in strips, it's good with salads, too.

But clearly there isn't space left to mention these things, or another helpful tidbit I had here somewhere, something to do to fresh corn on the cob. Still, there's not much reason to do anything to fresh corn on the cob. Because it's really very good the way it is. . . .

I was finishing this book on the front porch, glancing out occasionally at the long march of eucalyptus trees lining the beach, and the green-gray reach of the Pacific beyond. And suddenly the eucalyptus trees, with their strong trunks and forked branches and blossomy tops, looked like broccoli, and the ocean was turtle soup.

This is what can happen, all right. The whole matter of cooking can become intrusive, the kitchen itself looming larger than life-size.

But I think there's no need to let it. We'll just shut the tail gate quickly now, though gently, so that nothing jolts out, for it's time we all took off for wider horizons.

Index